A Project of the Fed

# Biblical Leadership After Moses

LESSONS TO BE LEARNED

Rabbi Charles Simon

Copyright © 2015 Federation of Jewish Men's Clubs, Inc.
ISBN 978-0-935665-09-3

# Biblical Leadership After Moses

## LESSONS TO BE LEARNED

*Written in honor of Dr. Burton (Captain Ruach) Fischman a continued source of guidance and inspiration.*

This book would never have seen fruition if it had not been for the support of the following organizations, Regions, and individuals.

- Laymen's Institute Alumni, New England Region, FJMC
- FJMC Foundation for Jewish Life
- The Internation Kiddush Club (IKC)
- The FJMC Midwest Region
- The FJMC Northern New Jersey Region
- Greg & Linda Gore
- The Gottesman Family
- Bart Kogan
- Stephen & Arlene Neustein
- Harold & Nancy Parritz
- Cantor Scott, Gail, Nadav, Haggai & Lily Simon
- Myles & Gail Simpson
- Tom & Michelle Sudow

# FORWARD

One of the hallmarks of the Federation of Jewish Men's Clubs has been the unwavering commitment to developing leaders within the ranks of its members. I have been an eyewitness to this extraordinary work over the past twenty-five years. Of course, there are many organizations that pay attention to leadership training. What makes the FJMC approach unique and compelling is its rootedness in the models of leadership that emanate from Torah.

This wonderful collection of essays offers principles of effective leadership for volunteers in any organization. Written by Rabbi Charles Simon, the long-serving, passionate and insightful leader of the FJMC men, these principles of leadership are clearly and persuasively detailed in a highly readable and accessible format.

For me, the most important leadership principle of all is the power of relationships. It is the relationship between leader and follower, chairperson and volunteer, that fuels any successful organization. When the leader makes the effort to know another's story, to discover the other's passions and talents, and to connect the other to the mission and purpose of the organization, there exists the possibility of what I have called "relational leadership." A relational leader earns the respect and trust of the volunteers when there is mutual personal disclosure, when stories are shared, when talents are combined to achieve a greater goal.

The FJMC has been blessed with extraordinary relational leaders. Over the years, I have met many of these amazing men who dedicate their lives to building the Jewish people through their volunteer work. They have been taught how to be Jewish leaders, how to infuse their volunteerism with Jewish values that are evident in these essays, with Jewish principles that animate the work of *tikkun olam* – perfecting the world, with Jewish enduring understandings that are the foundation of a powerful learning experience.

Moreover, the FJMC has embraced another crucial principle of relational leadership: the guys love each other. They care for each other. They are there for each other – in good times and in bad. When they are together, they do what real men who love each other do – they hug. They are attracted to their fantastic biennial conventions not just to learn from scholars and teachers; they come to be with each other, to learn from each other, to celebrate each other.

No one understands this more than Dr. Burt Fishman. He is known in the FJMC world as "Captain Ruach," the spiritual leader *par excellence*. To watch Burt whip up hundreds of guys into a frenzy of singing and dancing and celebration of the joys of being Jewish is to witness a leader who understands that it is one thing to tell people what to do, and it is quite another to be the model for others to emulate.

Thus, it is entirely fitting for this volume to be dedicated to Burt in honor of his many years of outstanding leadership. Burt is loved for his knowledge, his passion, and his singing, but mainly, he is loved because he loves: he loves his friends and colleagues, he loves the FJMC, he loves Judaism and Jewish living. *Yi'asher kochacha* to Burt and to the FJMC for teaching all of us the power of spirited relational leadership.

Dr. Ron Wolfson
Fingerhut Professor of Education
American Jewish University
Author, *Relational Judaism: Using the Power of Relationships to Transform the Jewish Community* (Jewish Lights Publishing)

# DEDICATION

This publication is dedicated in honor of Dr. Burton Fischman.

*Isn't he that guy that stands on the chair and gets everyone involved in a spirited Birkat Ha Mazon after meals?* Yes, he's the one. This very public face of our beloved Captain Ruach is known to anyone who has ever attended an FJMC event in New England, the Midwest or at FJMC's biennial convention. Burt has, in a very personal way, influenced, inspired and instructed an entire generation of Men's Club leaders. It is not an exaggeration to say that Burt's voice has touched each of us.

Burt had a distinguished career as a Professor of Communications at Bryant University in Smithfield, Rhode Island. He quickly became a popular motivational speaker and has written several books focusing on public speaking and leadership Burt served for many years as the Master of Ceremonies at the FJMC New England Region annual retreat, known then as the "Laymen's Institute". Just as there is much more behind the public Captain Ruach, describing Burt as simply the MC misses the extraordinary contribution that he made to ensure the success of the nation's oldest retreat for Jewish men.

Burt brought two key innovations to the planning of the Laymen's Institute that not only ensured that the event ran smoothly but by example taught the other members of the retreat team about leadership. The first is what became known as the *"megilla"*. This was in essence a minute-to-minute breakdown of the weekend and included not only the event title, but who was responsible for making it happen as well as what (if any) materials were needed for that particular item. Now many years after Burt left New England, the *"megilla"* retains its key role in planning for the retreat and developing future leaders for that event.

The second innovation is what became known as the *Laymen's Institute Manual of Operations,* still in use by FJMC. Essentially an extension of the *"megilla",* this manual identifies each step of the process of producing the Retreat and assigns a job title for that process. In this way, the manual not only ensures that nothing will fall between the cracks and be left undone, but creates a portal of entry for men to own a small part of the planning process. In so many cases, men who began with a limited role grew to accept more significant levels of responsibility and leadership.

For many years, Burt has been one of the central figures in FJMC training. Teaming with Norm Kurtz in the mid-1980s, Burt was one of the major architects of the FJMC's Joel Geffen Leadership Development Institute (LDI) which for the past two decades has served as the primary venue for training, motivating and inspiring future Men's Club leaders. To this day Burt, as the heart and soul of LDI, continues to inspire the men who have the privilege and opportunity to attend LDI. LDI would not be the same without the wit and passion of Captain Ruach.

At the age of 71, Burt and his wife Rhoda moved from their long-time home in New England and resettled in the Chicago area to be near one of their daughters and her family. To their delight, their second daughter recently moved to the Chicago/Milwaukee area as well. Many men would take advantage of this move to "hang up the cleats" but not Captain Ruach! Not only did Burt rapidly become a fixture of FJMC's Midwest Region and his local Men's Club, he embarked on a new career as a fitness trainer at the age of 80 and at age 84 he has returned to his early experiences as a song and dance man at the Catskills' resorts. Burt has once again reinvented himself and now provides invaluable and heartwarming entertainment experiences to hundreds of geriatric patients suffering from Alzheimer's and other forms of dementia. Burt was described as a "Motivating Spirit" by *The Chicago Jewish News* when recognized as one of the "Jewish Chicagoans of the Year" in 2013.

FJMC recognizes that leadership motivation and training is an ongoing process. That is why, to this day, each meeting of the international organization's executive leaders includes time for training led by Burt. In fact, in a perfect example of leadership development, Burt has "trained the trainers" so that some of these sessions are now also led by men who have been taught and motivated by the master himself. It is with affection, respect, and gratitude that this publication whose theme is leadership is dedicated to Burton Fischman, our own Captain Ruach!

BOB BRAITMAN AND NORM KURTZ

# TABLE OF CONTENTS

## Introduction | Leadership After Moses
AN INTRODUCTION TO LESSER KNOWN BIBLE STORIES | PG 11

### 1 Jepthah
THE CHALLENGE OF THE BEING A MAN OF HONOR | PG 17

### 2 Gideon
HERO OR NOT? | PG 23

### 3 Abimelech
ENFANTE TERRIBLE | PG 31

### 4 Jeroboam
THE MISJUDGED LEADER | PG 37

### 5 Jezebel
NOT THE WIFE OF YOUR DREAMS | PG 47

### 6 Hulda
THE PROPHET | PG 52

### 7 Josiah
THE GRAND RESTRUCTURING | PG 58

### 8 Manasseh The Conundrum
WHEN BAD THINGS HAPPEN TO GOOD PEOPLE | PG 65

### 9 Ezra and Nehemiah
RADICAL REFORMERS | PG 73

## Endgame | PG 85

# INTRODUCTION

# Leadership After Moses

## AN INTRODUCTION TO LESSER KNOWN BIBLE STORIES

---

After diligently watching the 2014 political debates, I concluded that I had wasted my time. None of the candidates had demonstrated leadership. None of the candidates provided a serious vision of what they would try to do. Instead, the conversations degenerated into pat phrases and mindless platitudes. What should have inspired me left me feeling anything but. People who watch political debates, regardless of whom they favor, hope to be moved. People who watch debates are looking for a leader. We hope for someone to inspire us and point the way toward a better future.

Dozens and dozens of books have been published in the past decade concerning leadership and management. Virtually every week I receive a flyer in the mail or an online solicitation that wants me to register for a course they claim will transform me into a more effective leader. Leadership journals and training programs are suddenly abundant in both the for-profit and not-for-profit sectors. There is widespread recognition that there is a lack of effective leadership.

Several of the biblical books after the five books of the Torah demonstrate the nature of and the development of leadership. The books of Samuel, Kings, and Judges are prime examples. These lessons are revealed through the stories of men (mostly) who either inherited positions of leadership or earned them in their own right within the context of a national religious framework. This framework, like the one in Judges, positions them in a potential relationship with God and depending upon their behaviors, whether they are either successful or unsuccessful, determines that relationship. This is important because the relationship of God to leaders reveals a core Jewish value that is almost always neglected or overlooked.

When it comes to leadership, God alone is viewed as the Ideal Leader; at its most basic level, Judaism is concerned that human leaders learn to understand and embody that ideal.

One of our great medieval sages, Saadia, understood the importance of leadership. He notes that,

> The highest object of human striving in this world ought to be eminence, majesty, and the occupation of a position of leadership….were it not for this aspiration toward leadership, there would have been no means of keeping the world in order or for looking after its welfare. (Saadia Gaon and Samuel Rosenblatt, The Book of Beliefs and Opinions, Yale, 1948)

The biblical book that is most concerned with leadership is the book of Judges. This book is a national religious record that begins immediately following the death of Joshua and concludes just prior to the birth of the last judge, Samuel. The characters within it reflect a variety of leadership styles and even include a detailed description of bad unconscionably corrupt leadership.

The book of Judges begins in the third generation after the exodus from Egypt and covers an alleged period of four hundred years (although historians seem to agree that it was more like two hundred years). The period of the judges ended with the coronation of King Saul in 1025 B.C.E.

What caused the development of the institution of judges?

Just prior to the dispersal of the tribes to their allocated lands and shortly before his death, Joshua brought the tribes together and through the instrument of a covenantal ceremony created a tribal confederacy. This compact committed the tribes to a mutual defense treaty similar to the Confederation of States agreement that united the original thirteen colonies prior to the writing of the U.S. Constitution. The book of Judges explains that during this period, God worked through specific men and women in Israel. It also informs us that following the death of Joshua the story and lessons of their common historical experience, of the liberation from slavery, the wandering in the desert and the receiving guidelines for a way of life, was forgotten or perhaps, not told. This is what the text tells us:

> Joshua son of Nun, the servant of the Lord died at the age of one hundred and ten years, and was buried on his own property, at Timnath-heres in the hill country of Ephraim, north of Mount Gaash. And all that generation were likewise gathered to their fathers. Another generation arose after them, which had not experienced the deliverance of the Lord or the deeds that he had wrought for Israel. And the Israelites did what was offensive to the Lord. They worshipped Baalim and forsook the Lord, the God of their fathers. (Judges 2:9-11)

At that time, Israel was in danger of being attacked from the north, south, and east, that is to say the Ammorites, Ammonites, Philistines, Sidionians and the Amalekites. It is doubtful that each of the tribes worshipped the same god. The Bible named their God or gods, Baalim, claiming that all of the gods of other peoples were a form of the god Baal.

This is important and will be further developed in the story of Gideon.

The book of Judges is a history of the men and women who assumed leadership positions in times of need, rallied the people against the encroaching enemies and lead them to victory. In most cases, as a result of their victories, the Bible tells us the men and women who led them "judged" the people for a certain amount of time afterwards and a period of peace prevailed.

Judges were charismatic men and women who, during times of need, suddenly appeared, performed some type of heroic deed and in doing so, served as one of the ways that God protected Israel. Gideon, Deborah, Samson, Jepthah and Samuel are the best known of the judges but there were others. There was Othniel the son of Caleb and Ehud the son of Gera, and Shamgar the son of Anath who slew six hundred Philistines with an ox-goad. There was Jair the Gileadite who led Israel for twenty-two years and there was Abimelech the son of Jerubbael (Gideon), whose story is most likely told to demonstrate that leaders can misuse and abuse their positions.

The Tribal Confederacy, like the Confederation of States, had serious flaws. These flaws were reflected in a statement which is constantly repeated in the book of Judges,

> At that time there was no King in Israel and every man did as he thought right. (e.g. Judges 17:6)

Theoretically speaking, the children of Israel didn't need a King because God was their King. But, depending upon the reader's point of view, either because they ignored "the ways of their fathers" or because of the political nature of the time, they were forced to develop a form of government which would protect them from hostile invasion and would preserve their emerging way of life.

The essays and stories that follow were selected to both educate about a period in biblical history which is often overlooked and to raise questions about leadership from the Bible's authors' points of view. I have added one additional story that is not from Judges, Samuel or Kings. It's a more modern story and is extracted from the third section of the Bible, the books of Ezra and Nehemiah. Their story reflects two different approaches to leadership and a challenge which most of us have to face.

A few final notes specifically because it is applicable to the way Burt Fischman has been conducting himself for the past thirty plus years. Today, perhaps more than ever, organizations are finding that fewer and fewer people are willing to accept positions of leadership. This goes against the grain of Jewish tradition. The Midrash Tanhuma on parshat Mishpatim (Exodus 21-24) comments that people must not remove themselves from positions of leadership or shy away from assuming that responsibility.

It strengthens this statement with the following illustration:

> When Rabbi Assi was dying, his nephew saw him weeping. He said, "Why do you weep? Is there any part of the Law which you have not learnt? Your disciples sit before you. Is there any deed of loving kindness which you have not done? And over and above all these qualities, you have kept yourself far from the judge's office, and you have not brought it over yourself to be appointed as an official for the needs of the community."
>
> He replied, "That is why I weep. Perhaps, I shall have to give an account because I was able to be a judge and did not judge. A man who retires to his house and says, "What have I to do with the burden on the community, or with their suits," Why should I listen to their voice? Peace to thee, O my soul-such a one destroys the world."

For more than thirty years, Burt has read the texts, piloted the models, and demonstrated the necessary behaviors to show us that this trend can be countered. He has taught us that leadership takes many forms and that leadership can be developed. It can be learned.

Some people are driven to be leaders. Others lead in different ways. There are dynamic leaders, visionary leaders, servant leaders, spiritual leaders, militant leaders and there are times when leadership is suddenly thrust upon someone. Not everyone desires to be a leader but there times in everyone's lives, in everyone's families when one has to lead.

One thing is for certain, "Leadership is not Governance!" Roseamund Stone Zander and Benjamin Zander say in their book, *The Art of Possibility,* (Boston, Harvard business School Press 2000, pp.68-73.)

> The conductor of an orchestra does not make a sound. His picture may appear on the cover of the CD in various dramatic poses, but his true power derives from his ability to make other people powerful... The activity of leadership is not limited to conductors, presidents and the player who energizes the orchestra is exercising leadership of the most profound kind.

In the volunteer and leisure worlds, people often assume positions of leadership without knowing why. Maybe it just felt like the right thing to do, or a sudden urge to make a difference suddenly manifested itself. Perhaps, like those in Judges, they responded to an inner voice. They were "called". Perhaps, like many of us they could have chosen to not respond to that inner voice. But they did. They volunteered as do we. As Burt has taught us.

# 1

# Jepthah

## THE CHALLENGE OF BEING A MAN OF HONOR

*Jepthah is the fourth major character mentioned in the book of Judges. He was preceded by Deborah who is named a prophet, Gideon, and his son Abimelech. When reading this essay, ask yourself "How would you define his leadership style? What were his strengths and what were his weaknesses?" Finally, what are the lessons that the authors of this text wished us to learn?*

One of the most interesting stories in the book of Judges is the story of Jepthah, (Judges 10:6-12:70). Part of his story is summarized in the haftarah (the prophetic portion) which is read corresponding to parshat Hukkat (Numbers 19:1-22). Jepthah was a charismatic leader afflicted with classical flaws.

He was the son of a Gideonite man and a prostitute and as a result was ridiculed and scorned by his brothers from birth. He was always mistreated and his step mother and brothers were able to successfully deny him his rightful inheritance. He was kind of a Cinderfella. As a result of the way his family and the people of

Gideon treated him, he developed into what we would call today an "unsavory character" and eventually was forced to flee to the hill country, a place referred to as "Tob". Tob was the place where the criminals and exiles who had been banished went to live. It was a rough and dangerous place.

Apparently he had leadership abilities and over time gathered men of a similar nature to his side. They made a living by raiding farms and stealing from caravans. Unlike Robin Hood he stole from everyone and kept everything.

Sometime later the villages of Gideon came under attack from the Ammonites. Lacking any militia, the Gideonites reached out to Jepthah since he was the only person with what was essentially a private army, and begged him to lead them into battle. Jepthah reminded them of the way he had been treated in the past and indicated that if he defended them he desired to be compensated.

The people agreed and promised that if he led them to victory they would acknowledge him as their leader. Jepthah bargained with the elders of Gilead in the same manner that David, in the not too distant future, would negotiate to obtain the crown of Israel. Jepthah didn't fully trust the elders of Gilead however, and he only agreed to serve as their military leader if the elders and the people of Gilead went to the holy place of Mitzpah and swore in front of the Lord that they would honor the terms of the agreement. Mitzpah, like Shiloh, was among the holy places in Israel before they were replaced by Jerusalem.

Vows, both private and public, were considered to be binding in those days. One couldn't retract a vow.

Jepthah understood how damaging a war could be and rather than immediately attack, his first act as a leader was to attempt to negotiate. He sent messengers to the Ammonite King and attempted to learn why they were attacking. The King of the Ammonites claimed the land of Gideon belonged to them and that they were displaced some three hundred years ago. Messengers went back and forth and unfortunately, the situation escalated. At what point did Jepthah ask

"To whom does this land truly belong?"

Diplomacy failed and eventually degenerated into a shouting match. Jepthah lost his temper and jeeringly claimed that the god of the Ammonites couldn't protect his lands and that it hadn't been in their possession for nearly 300 years. "And by the way, why haven't you tried to reclaim this land before?" Of course the ramifications of who is the rightful owner of parts of Israel have yet to be resolved, but that's not part of this story.

Some things just don't change and the failure of diplomacy resulted in war. Jepthah made plans for his army to march through Gilead and Manasseh, and into the Ammonite territory.

Just before the battle, Jepthah, like David, sealed the deal with his people before God that is with an oath made in God's name in a shrine, a place dedicated to God's worship. Jepthah also made a personal vow.

Vows were and are very important. In those days, people were judged by their words. When someone made a promise, the worst thing they could do was to break it. It would ruin their reputation. In those days, and in many circles today people are extremely careful what they say about others because on some level they know that words have power.

The Talmud tells us that saying the wrong thing about a person can be likened to murder. Vows were so important that an entire book of the Talmud is devoted to learning about vows. We always need to be careful about what we say.

Today, when people in power who have legitimate authority, like mayors, Senators or a President make statements, they are held to and judged by their words. The more powerful the person, the more impact the words. When a biblical ruler made a vow, a really important vow, he made it to God. Abraham and Isaac and Jacob did it and so did Jepthah. This is what he vowed:

If you deliver the Ammonites into my hands, then whatever comes out of the door of my house to meet me on my safe return from the Ammonites shall be the Lord's and shall be offered by me as a burnt offering. (Judges 10:30-31) This story has parallels in the Greek and Roman mythology where heroes often suffer personal tragedies for unaccountable reasons. If anything the story reminds us to be careful, especially after success, when one can be so flushed with joy that he or she does foolish things. In this case the outcome was tragic.

What could he have been thinking? In those days people believed that it was their responsibility to offer birds and cows and sheep and fruits and vegetables, all sorts of things to God, either as a way of thanking God or as a way to obtain God's attention so that protection and prosperity would result. Jepthah might have remembered that Abraham was prepared to sacrifice Isaac to God. If he remembered that story he probably remembered that God didn't wanted humans sacrificed and so he might have figured that a cat or a dog would be the first being to run out of the house to greet him, and if he happened to be wrong and was a person, that God would most likely forgive him.

But he was wrong.

The next portion of the story is found in the haftarah for Hukkat, (Judges 11:1-33), but, the haftarah omits a significant, perhaps the most significant part of the story. The first person to cross his threshold was his daughter. When Jepthah returned home his daughter, his only daughter ran out of the house dancing and singing and playing an instrument called a timbrel. "Daddy's home! Daddy's home", she sang.

Jepthah screams and mourns. He fell on his knees crying. He ripped his clothes as a sign of mourning and tearfully said,

> O daughter, you have brought me low; you have become my troubler. For I have vowed a vow to the Lord and can't take it back. (Judges 11:35)

(The word, "troubler" is called "achor" in Hebrew. This is important because in the book of Joshua, Joshua executes a man who took the spoils from the city of Jericho in the valley of Achor. The victim's act severed a treaty that Joshua had made with God and apparently God was so enraged that he stopped the conquest dead in its tracks until Joshua straightened things out. The word, "achor" is a literary reminder of the consequences that one would incur if they violated a promise made to God.)

And she replied,

> Father, you have made a vow to the Lord and the Lord has made you victorious. I know you can't take it back but grant me two months and I will go with my companions and prepare myself and come to grips with the fact that I will never know the joys of love as a grown up. (Judges 11:36-38)

Two months later, she returned and he did to her as he had vowed. And it became a custom in Israel for the maidens in the community to chant sad songs in her memory for four days on the anniversary of her death, year after year.

It is possible that the authors of this story didn't understand Jepthah's sacrifice of his daughter as a failure of leadership but instead understood it as a model for successful leadership. Some historians claim that the people of the time expected a leader to honor his or her vows to God and to be willing to sacrifice anything in order to succeed. Perhaps, just as Abraham was willing to sacrifice his son and would have, if divine intervention had not occurred, Jepthah hoped to be able to avert the necessary but severe vow that he had made. Unfortunately, in this instance, God didn't negotiate or forgive.

This story is an early indication that the tribal confederacy wasn't providing sufficient defense against the neighboring tribes. It was the first of many indications that a more central form of government was needed.

*The story of Jepthah speaks to us on a national religious level and also a personal one. In its context in the book of Judges it teaches us about the need for a workable form of government and that in biblical times, a country governed by a king provided defense and the opportunity for peace.*

*On the more personal level, it challenges us to consider the nature of the promises we make, the language we use, and the consequences of our actions. It reminds us that we need to honor our words, no matter how difficult that may be, and that our leaders also need to remember to whom they are responsible.*

# 2

## Gideon

### HERO OR NOT?

*Gideon is the pivotal and perhaps the most complicated figure in the book of Judges. His story raises a number of questions many of which cannot be answered. The Bible is promoting the need for a King, a just and responsible ruler. Gideon could possibly fill that role but doesn't appear to be able to overcome the stumbling blocks that have been placed in his way.*

*The Bible understands judges to be leaders but not necessarily leaders with kingly ability. Gideon was an inspired leader and his leadership style suggests much which should be learned. But if we evaluate the period when he served as a Judge and analyzed the decisions he made shouldn't we ask was he successful? Was he compromised, did his personal goals override his vision and if they did what do we need to know to avoid his errors?*

Two of the most interesting and complicated stories in the Book of Judges are the stories of Gideon and his son Abimelech. These stories raise a number of questions that specifically pertain to different styles of leadership and at the same time shed light on the complexities of leaders and those who strive to more fully understand them. Gideon is the pivotal figure in the book of Judges. He was the last judge where the term, "the land was at peace" or the "land rested for forty years", was used. He was also the last judge to whom God appears in some form until the birth of Samuel.

There is a consensus among scholars that in the final form of the book, Judges is composed of two different sets of tales: the initial five stories preceding the tale of Abimelech and the seven following. The initial five tales record the judges' successes and those following the tale of Abimelech, including Jepthah and Samson recount the tales of leaders (judges) who suffered from serious character flaws.

One can understand the Gideon's story on two levels. The first level is structural. It is a story composed of four parts: the development of Gideon's faith, the connection of God to the Exodus, the destruction of the local shrine, and finally, the angelic revelation. Gideon's story reflects his path to belief, followed by a conversion, (yes, conversion), which leads to assuming a position of leadership. The story raises a number of questions about the need for national leadership and how one responds when great opportunities are presented.

The second level of the Gideon story operates on is the cosmic one. It is the story of the Israelite God's triumph over Baal.

This story was probably composed in the late ninth to early eighth century B.C.E. This was the time of Hosea. This was the time of Elijah and his battle against the prophets of Baal. This was the time of Queen Jezebel and her husband Ahab who reintroduced Baal worship into northern Israel. This was the period just prior to the Assyrian destruction of the Northern Kingdom.

Yes, a lot was going on. The Kingdom of Judah (Jerusalem) continued to be ruled by the descendants of King David and was constantly in conflict with the Northern Kingdom of Israel that had seceded and formed its own kingdom after the death of King Solomon. The Northern Kingdom lasted for nearly two hundred years. Its greatest weakness was its failure to establish the necessary dynastic security which was crucial for the survival of a nation. As a result the Northern Kingdom was governed by a succession of dynasties and ruled by whoever was able to rise to power and supplant his predecessor at any particular time.

This was also the time when our notion of one God, a God of Israel with many names, began to emerge. On the cosmic level God, YHWH, was fighting and conquering and eventually supplanting the local tribal gods. This is the time when the concept of the ideal leader, ruler, and king emerged.

(But more of that later).

In order to understand the issues of leadership presented in Gideon's story, we need understand a little more about the Northern Kingdom. While the Bible is less than enthusiastic about the Northern kingdom, the historically reality was that it was more populated and more prosperous than the Southern kingdom, Israel- Jerusalem in the 8th century. At that time, Jerusalem was most likely a small town, surrounded by a few villages, and existed perhaps a little above the poverty level. The Northern kingdom was situated on the trade routes and was composed of a series of fertile valleys with sufficient water to grow and export a number of crops.

The authors of our text, living hundreds of years later, most likely in Babylon, were concerned with the return to Israel and idealizing the past. In order to convince the exiled population to return and support life in Israel, they developed a message which stressed the importance of the Davidic kingdom and the importance of Jerusalem. They created an image of Jerusalem, the golden city as the capital of the ancient world. In reality it was never more than a satrap, a vassal state to any number of a series of empires.

As a result, the epic story of God battling and triumphing over Baal and other local gods which eventually were merged into the God of the Jewish people, a god with many names, (El, Shaddai, Elohim and of course YHWH) reflected the need to demonstrate YHWH's supremacy. The story of Gideon on the cosmic level demonstrates God's victory over Baal.

Let's unravel Gideon's story. He is the only hero mentioned in the book of Judges who converted to Yahwism and who actually needed to do so before qualifying as a leader.

This is his story. It is found in Judges Chapters 6-8.

Gideon apparently had heard about how YHWH (the national God) worked wonders in Egypt. But that isn't enough to convince him to abandon the faith of his birth. Gideon is the only hero or Judge who asks for miraculous signs and questions God's commitment. He is also the only hero in the book with two names one of them implying he worshipped Baal.

The Israelites (Northern Kingdom) were harried by the Midianites for seven years, allegedly, according to our text, because the Israelites had abandoned God.

> Israel was reduced to utter misery by the Midianites, and the Israelites cried out to the Lord. (Judges 6:6)

Gideon, is visited by one of God's messengers, an angel who tells him,

> The Lord is with you valiant warrior. (Judges 6:12)

Gideon, who has heard about this God is doubtful questions the angel and asks if that's so, where are all the wondrous deeds which our fathers told us about. Where are the miracles like we had in Egypt? As a result the Lord demonstrates God's power until Gideon realizes with whom he is dealing. Gideon is then instructed to tear down Baal's altar and post (Asherah) that his father had built and to construct a new altar dedicated to the Lord.

The following morning the townspeople wake up and realize their altar had been desecrated. They learn that Gideon was the culprit and they seek to have him killed. Gideon's father, Joash, responds to the townspeople with the words,

> If Baal is a God, let him fight his own battles.(Judges 6:31)

From that point onward, Gideon, who now believes in the God of Israel, is referred to as Jerubaal, possibly meaning "Let Baal fight with him".

Let's recap. We have the father of an Israelite hero, a member of a Northern Israelite tribe, who lives in the town of Ophrah and who practiced polytheism. He kept an altar to Baal and an Asherah (image or post) and he gave his son a Baalist name. The author of Judges could not write a story about a hero chosen by God to drive out the Midianites whose name was associated with Baal. So they possibly devised the name "Gideon." Gideon comes from the root *gada*, which means *to cut down*. This phrase is also found in Deuteronomy 7:5 where it means *to cut down sacred posts*. Sacred posts were part of cult of goddess Asherah.

The Lord fills Gideon with his spirit and he reaches out to the neighboring tribes and calls for aid and they respond affirmatively. And we ask, "Was he chosen to be a leader or did circumstances place him in a position of leadership?" That's almost always the question isn't it?

Gideon knew what to say and the people rallied to him. He prepared for battle and gathered an army of thirty-two thousand men. But the Lord or the authors of our story wasn't satisfied with this response. We are told that the Lord demands he reduces his forces to three hundred. Gideon arms his soldiers with pitchers and horns and without weapons of war they conquer the Midianites and pursue them. Gideon and the Lord have been victorious.

The tribe of Ephraim, concerned about their status with the other tribes, was offended because they were not invited to the battle. At which point Gideon demonstrates that a leader needs to be diplomatic. He calms the Ephraimites and prevents a civil war. After avoiding the conflict with Ephraim, he leads his men across the Jordan and pursues the remaining Midianites and their kings,

Zebah and Zalmunna. His men, famished from the battle and the pursuit, enter the village of Sukkoth and later the village of Penuel and request food and water. In both instances they were refused.

Gideon's response to this snubbing seemed somewhat out of character from the man who just avoided a war by being diplomatically savvy. He became incensed, arrogant and he swore upon returning that he would torture the elders of Sukkoth and tear down the tower of Penuel. And that's exactly what he did.

> He took the elders of the city and brought desert thorns and briers. He punished the people of Sukkoth with them. As for Penuel, he tore down its tower and killed the townspeople. (Judges 8:16-17)

Gideon's behavior makes one wonder if this is the way a messenger of the Lord, a Judge, should behave? When Deborah condemned those who did not participate in the battle with Sisera; she did not inflict personal harm. Gideon might have been a Judge but in this instance he acted like a despot. What caused him to respond so violently? Was his behavior justifiable?

What kind of leader is governed by ego?

> Then he came to the people of Sukkot and said, "Here are Zebah and Zalmunna, about whom you mocked me. (Judges 8:15)

This is where the story of Gideon becomes interesting. The book of Judges, clearly desires a King, one who rules in the spirit of the Lord. Gideon, has clearly risen to a position of authority at a time when a King was needed to protect the tribes. Yet the text clearly tells us that when offered the kingship, Gideon explicitly refused.

Then the men of Israel said to Gideon, Rule over us-you, your son and your grandson as well; for you have saved us from the Midianites. But Gideon replied; I will not rule over you myself, nor shall my son rule over you; the

Lord alone shall rule over you. (Judges 8:22-23)

One would think the text is helping us to understand that leadership can be temporary and that one does not require a title to have influence and yield authority. Gideon actually, might have been a worthy candidate because he realized kingship belonged to God.

But his actions were problematic. He could have just been giving lip service. Maybe he secretly desired to be King but knew the only way to achieve that goal was to refuse the peoples' offer. Some of his actions were kinglike. Some of his behaviors were clearly autocratic and not reflective of the behaviors of an ideal leader.

Sovereignty must have been on his mind.

Listen to how the Kings of Midian describes his family.

> Then he asked Zebah and Zalmunna, "Those men you killed at Tabor, what were they like? They looked just like you, they replied, like sons of a king. They were my brothers, he declared, the sons of my mother. As the Lord lives, if you had spared them, I would not kill you. And he commanded his oldest son Jether "go kill them" But the boy did not draw his sword, for he was timid and still a boy." (Judges 8:18-20)

He acted like a king when he tortured Sukkoth and massacred the people of Penuel. He also ordered his eldest son to execute the Midianite kings. Did he do that so he could learn if his son had what it takes to rule?

Gideon might have refused to become king because he desired to establish a dynasty. After declining the offer he requests the earring's of the conquered peoples and the crescents and pendants and the purple robes worn by the Kings of Midian. He gathers gold from the people and creates a cultic object. He creates an ephod, an object with holy implications.

Aaron, Moses's brother, the high priest, wore an ephod. In this instance the ephod was apparently a pillar. The medieval commentator Rashi claimed it was built as a reminder to the nation that their victory had been miraculous.

But could it have meant something else? The author of the story blames Gideon for leading Israel into sin and believed that the presence of the ephod clouded Gideon's and the people's motivation. Instead of serving as a memorial of the Lord's victory it became an object of veneration. They began to worship and immediately afterwards *all Israel went astray.*

Gideon behaved like a king. He had seventy sons and many wives. One son, his youngest, was born from a concubine in Shechem and was named (Abimelech) my father is king. Gideon had become more than just a simple wheat farmer from Ophrah.

It could be that Gideon, the newly converted, the person within the spirit of the Lord initially resided, acted initially as an ideal ruler should. Perhaps he had the ability to become the idealized king. And perhaps success tarnished his persona and the spirit left him, left him to his own devises and he reverted to what he once was: a person who created or who worshipped idols and placed the personal and family gain over the larger more ambitious goals that leaders of nations should have.

*The story of Gideon challenges us to learn that leadership qualities can slip and are easily abused. But if we wish to understand more about abusive destructive leadership we need to learn the story of the son of Jerubbaal, Abimelech.*

# 3

## The Story of Abimelech

### THE ENFANTE TERRIBLE

*The Story of Abimelech begins at the end of Judges, Chapter 8 and concludes at the end of Chapter 9. When reading this essay, consider the nature of people who strive for power and position. How should one relate to them? How should one conduct oneself around the Abimelech's of this world?*

*The story as if it was told by his uncle:*

My name is Merubabel, brother of Joash and uncle of the one who is referred to as Gideon/Jerubbaal. It is my unfortunate duty to tell the story of my nephew's folly, one that was responsible for the ruin of our family. My nephew, Gideon, was a quite a leader in his early years. Unfortunately, as he aged, after having turned down the office of King of the Northern tribes, his behavior was more kinglike than it should have been. He fathered many, many children, the book of Judges employs the term "seventy", which was its way of saying this guy was very active, and of course had many, many wives.

He also had a concubine. I can't remember her name. She must have been something, an unusual beauty, because with seventy wives how could anyone find the time?

It must have happened on one of his visits to offer sacrifice when the Ark of the Tabernacle was residing at Schechem. Perhaps he had been travelling alone or stopped at a local inn and there she was. The result - another son. He named him Abimelech. What could he have been thinking? Abimelech means "My father is king!" If Gideon was opposed to the monarchy why would he have given that name to his son?

I can't help but wonder if Gideon gave the boy that name in order to compensate for his illegitimate birth. Perhaps, he was a love child and this was only way he could compensate for not having him fully recognized.

The story of Abimelech raises more questions than it answers. I remember hearing how he went to the people in the town of his birth and convinced them to agree that they would prefer being ruled by one person than all of the sons of Jerubbaal. He reminded them that he is his mother's, (a local resident) son.

The people of Shechem identified with him and provided him with funding. He used the money to hire a small army of "worthless and reckless fellows", with whom he journeyed to Ophrah and proceeded to slaughter all but one of Gideon's sons, who escaped and went into hiding. This son's name was Jotham. He was Abimelech's younger half-brother.

The people of Shechem were ecstatic. They proclaimed Abimelech "King". When Jotham came out of hiding and heard about this, he journeyed to Shechem and urged the people to remember that his father had saved them from the Midianites. He pleaded with them to reconsider their decision and to act justly. It was too little too late. Jotham made his pitch and fled.

The honeymoon of kingship lasted for three years and then things went sour. The people of Shechem either rethought their loyalty or became fed up with the way their king was behaving. They formed a blockade and began to appropriate the goods carried by caravans and traders. Today we call this "imposing sanctions." By refusing to allow caravans and traders to bring their products into Shechem, they undermined Abimelech's economic base and empowered local chieftains. This further exacerbated the situation.

These actions must not have been sufficient or Abimelech must have responded harshly because the people of Shechem also engaged a mercenary band lead by Gaal the son of Ebed to get rid of him. It was a local rebellion and when the city's governor, Zebul heard about it, he messengered Abimelech and arranged to ambush Gaal and his troops. Gaal was defeated and Abimelech remained in Shechem to make sure that another rebellion wouldn't occur.

I am ashamed to even think that he was even remotely related to me. He was a spiteful, vicious bastard. He surrounded the people with his army, recaptured the city and massacred all of the people in it. He razed the town to the ground and sowed it with salt.

When the people of the neighboring village, either called Millo, or the tower of Schechem, heard about the slaughter they hid in a tunnel. Abimelech and his soldiers, set fire to the tunnel and killed every man, woman and child. Estimates were difficult, but I heard more than one thousand people died that day. What a terrible way to die.

The bloodlust must have come upon him because he marched to Thebez the neighboring fortified town. I have no idea why after having subdued Millo and Schechem he continued the purge. Perhaps his army required more plunder? Perhaps he just enjoyed the carnage. Fearing for their lives, the people of Thebez locked themselves in the tower. Abimelech prepared to put it to the torch but fortunately for the people of Thebez just as he was about to set the tower's door on fire, a woman dropped a millstone on his head which cracked his skull. I suspect he was afraid of being tortured. He called out for his death and his aide promptly took his life.

Everyone had had enough. They went home hoping to rebuild.

The story of Abimelech found in the book of Judges is unique. In order for us to understand it in all of its complexity it needs to be viewed from a number of different perspectives. First of all, Abimelech was not a judge, he was an alleged king; yet his story is almost in the exact middle of the book. Unlike most of the judges he wasn't called by God but rose to power by appealing to popular will, hiring mercenaries, and eliminating rivals through murder. Abimelech's grasp for power defied the current social norms. He attempted to establish his right to rule through his mother's family while the standard norms of ancient Israel and surrounding nations accepted patrilineal kingship.

Unlike the other judges he didn't deliver Israel from anything. There was no external enemy. And his story ends without the expected reference to Israel being delivered, or the number of years he served as a Judge. Instead notice is given that his fate was a divine repayment for his wickedness. If one analyzes the judges whose stories precede and follow his story, one learns that the early judges, up to Gideon all received some type of divine inspiration. Gideon was the last judge to have these types of visions.

Now that we've read the story in his words, there are some observations.

If Abimelech wasn't a judge, why was his story included in the book? One possible reason could be that the story served to demonstrate the authors' objection to the monarchy. Another possible reason could be that both the Gideon and Abimelech stories were not about kingship but were more concerned with how leaders are chosen. *This is an important point, Leaders can be chosen! But what do they require to be effective?*

There are some who believe that the stories were included in the book as criticisms of a specific form of monarchy that existed at the time. The Northern Kingdom (called Israel) existed for approximately two hundred years and was characterized by a series of revolutions and rebellions while the Davidic kingdom in the South was a stable and long lasting dynasty. Standing at center of the book of Judges, the Abimelech narrative disposes of the idea that there might be a royal alternative to the Davidic dynasty.

But didn't the book and period of the Judges precede the birth and rise of David? How is it possible that an anti-Northern polemic could have been written?

There are two ways this can be understood. In the first instance the story could reinforce the reason why the Davidic dynasty was elevated at the expense of house of Saul. Saul was a Benjaminite, a representative from the North. As King, David did everything possible to eliminate the possibilities of Saul's family ever regaining any influence. Abimelech was from the first capital of the Northern kingdom, Shechem, the place where Jeroboam, the first northern king, established his capital.

There is another possibility; one which impresses me tremendously and in one sense opens a window into the brilliance of our holy texts but through a non-theological lens. Consider our ancestors, the scholars living in Babylon during the exile who were tasked, or who voluntarily assumed the task of constructing the books we call the Tanakh, the Bible.

These people wove together stories and incidents which were ancient and coupled them with a Divine imperative. One of these imperatives was to empower people who came from the province of Judea more than one hundred years earlier, who had settled and acculturated into the most sophisticated society of the time, to desire to return to their promised land. Part of this imperative was to rebuild a country and to reestablish a time of prosperity and peace. It couldn't have been the Northern Kingdom which only lasted two hundred odd years and was destroyed in 721 B.C.E. by the Assyrians.

It had to be the Southern Kingdom, the Kingdom of David, the kingdom eternal the Kingdom of Solomon and his descendants. The people who wove these stories together skillfully crafted positive encouragements about the Kingdom of David and equally so, shaped their feelings about the corrupt, contentious, idolatrous kingdom in the north. The Northern tribes were always rebelling, the Northern tribes were always abandoning their God and backsliding and worshipping false gods. The Northern people were the ones with whom the prophets cautioned and warned of their imminent destruction.

The editors of our texts succeeded in stages over hundreds of years, in producing a magnificent work. Each segment, the Torah, the Prophets or the Writings emphasized the importance of David, Jerusalem and yes, even the Priesthood. Within this grand context, *the authors of the Book of Judges, a book concerned with the need for a proper ideal form of leadership, told the story of a person with the wrong ideas who forced his way to kingship. People who seek office for the wrong reasons, according to our book, often fail because even though we have free will, there are times when according to the text God permits this to occur.*

# 4

# Jeroboam

## THE MISJUDGED LEADER

*Jeroboam's story is found in I Kings, Chapters 11-16. He is one of the most misjudged leaders in the Bible. The authors of our text and the rabbis who followed considered him to be one of the most despicable characters in our history. But was that the case? Ask yourself how is he depicted in the story? Is he portrayed as charismatic, thoughtful, strategically orientated leader or as a self-serving idolater? Consider how he is presented and evaluate his alleged flaws.*

The Bible is filled with the stories of outstanding personalities. Some of them were heroes and others; while others were and are considered something other. Most of us know the story of Haman and some of us recall the story of Korah both of whom were considered undesirable, to say the least. But very few of us know the story of Jeroboam the son of Nebat, who is described in the Bible and the Talmud as one of the most reviled personalities in our history. His infamy was only rivaled by that of a King named Manasseh who lived one hundred years before the Babylonian conquest.

Jeroboam is credited by the authors of I Kings with organizing the rebellion against Solomon's heir, Rehoboam, and splitting the nation into two. According to the book's authors, in addition to splitting the Kingdom he was ultimately responsible for the Assyrian empire's conquest of the Northern Kingdom. The authors of Kings I described the form of worship which he instituted as idolatrous and pagan, the exact opposite of what they understood God would desire. As a result of his activities, every Northern King who followed him, regardless of their ability and successes, were judged as illegitimate and were despised in the authors or redactors eyes. If David represented the ideal king, Jeroboam reflected the exact opposite. But if we read his story, a different picture begins to emerge.

The reasons for the nation of Judah splitting into two separate countries in 928 B.C.E. and the reasons Jeroboam is reviled in our tradition, are more complex than the story the Bible tells. Understand this split requires a basic understanding of the politics surrounding the rise and reign of King David as well as the ideological thrust of the redactors of Deuteronomy. The alleged incident that caused the division of Solomon's kingdom into Judah and Israel is recorded in I Kings, Chapter 12.

The story begins when Rehoboam, Solomon's son and successor, journeys to the holy city of Shechem to be crowned by the tribes. This in itself is surprising and indicative of the tension which existed between either the Northern tribes and the Southern tribes or the tribes and the monarchy, because one would have assumed that the coronation would take place in the nation's capital, Jerusalem. But it didn't. Shechem must have been a compromise.

At Shechem the assembled tribes acknowledged they would accept Rehoboam as their king if he lightened the burdens that Solomon had imposed. Solomon had heavily taxed the Northern tribes in order to pay for the Temple's construction. He had further conscripted their men to serve in his armies. The text does not shed any light on the tension that must have arisen when Solomon constructed the Temple that looked like a Phoenician place of worship thus ignoring the traditional tent shrine style that had existed since the time of

Moses. One supposes that the animosity of the tribes also increased when he proclaimed Jerusalem, a place where tribal authority was non-existent, to be the center of the nation. Suffice it to say, the construction of the Temple was the most controversial moment in the young nation's history.

The establishment of a Temple in a city devoid of tribal traditions and the transporting of the Ark of the Covenant to Jerusalem, coupled with the changes which occurred in the international arena created opposition from the old religious centers which still played a vital role in the people's lives.

Had the international climate not changed, Solomon still would have had his hands full. But unfortunately, a new dynasty emerged in Egypt in 945 B.C.E. which was hostile to Solomon and to Israel's role in the international scene. The Egyptian rulers sought to weaken Israel's influence in the ancient world by encouraging rebellions and breakaways in Solomon's kingdom extremities. These efforts were successful and the economy of Israel, already burdened with huge debts to other nations, was further weakened. The loss of trade routes and diminishing markets shifted Israel's balance of trade from a positive balance to a negative one. In order to pay his debts to Hiram of Tyre (who had provided him with men and necessary raw materials to build the Temple) Solomon was forced to cede control of twenty cities from Akko in the south to Tyre in the north.

The Bible tells a different story, explaining that these calamities were God's punishment for allowing Solomon's alien wives to introduce idolatrous cults into the court. (I Kings 11:14).

These factors were all in play when Solomon's son, Rehoboam, sought to become king. Most likely the move from Jerusalem to Shechem was an act of appeasement. Shechem was the major city directly North of Jerusalem on the north-south highway near the border of the most powerful northern tribes, Ephraim and Manasseh.

Rehoboam met with the tribes twice. Initially, they indicated they were willing to accept his sovereignty if he reduced their taxes. Rehoboam dismissed them and requested they return again in three days. During this period he took counsel with two groups of advisors, his father's counselors and his friends. The former group advised to treat the people kindly, the latter to treat them harshly.

> And the young men with whom he had grown up answered, "My father imposed a heavy yoke on you, and I will add to your yoke; my father flogged you with whips, but I will flog you with scorpions. (I Kings 12:11)

At this point, according to the text, the ten tribes seceded and we are informed that Jeroboam returned from Egypt because the text states that:

> ...upon hearing that he had returned the tribes sent messengers to him and summoned him to a tribal assembly and made him king. (I Kings 12:20)

Enter Jeroboam.

Prior to the debacle at Shechem and the splitting of the nation, Chapter 11 introduces us to the man who appears to be the hero of our story.

> Jeroboam son of Nebat, an Ephraimite of Zeredah was in Solomon's service ...This Jeroboam was an able man, and when Solomon saw that the young man was a capable worker, he appointed him over all the forced labor of the House of Joseph.(I Kings 11:26,28)

It appears that Jeroboam was a leader with tremendous potential but inserted in between these statements in verse 11:27 is a revealing phrases,

> The circumstances under which he raised his hand against the king are as follows...

In the next section, verses 29-36:

> ...During that time Jeroboam went out of Jerusalem and the prophet Ahijah met him on the way. He had put on a new robe; and when the two

of them were alone in the open country, Ahijah took hold of the new robe and tore it into twelve pieces. Take ten pieces," he said to Jeroboam. "For thus said the Lord, the God of Israel: I am about to tear the kingdom out of Solomon's hands and I will give you ten tribes. For they have forsaken Me; they have worshiped Ashtoreth the goddess of the Phoenicians, Chemosh the god of Moab, and Milcom the god of the Ammonites; they have not walked in My ways or done what is pleasing to Me, as his father David did. But one tribe will remain his for the sake of my servant David and for the sake of Jerusalem, the city I have chosen.

This certainly seems like plotting rebellion, meeting in the country with a northern Prophet who was anything but a supporter of the King. Imagine how Jeroboam must have reacted when he learned that Solomon had word of this secret rendezvous. Fearing for his life he fled to Egypt where he was welcomed by the new anti-Solomon Egyptian King, Shishak. He remained in exile until Solomon's death. Was it possible that Jeroboam and Ahijah were one of many groups of people who were fed up with Solomon's punitive policies?

As Bob Dylan famously sang,

> Something is happening here but you don't know what it is…

But who was this mysterious prophet named Ahijah?

Ahijah was a Levite prophet from Shiloh. This is important because both David and Jeroboam came from the vicinity of Shiloh. In I Samuel 17:12, David is referred to as being from Bethlehem and an "Ephratite" which could mean a person from Ephraim, a phrase which is also used when describing Samuel's birthplace near Shiloh.

Ahijah's priestly, Levitical status was also a significant factor. Towards the end of David's reign, David appointed a priest to guide him. This priest came from a different, non-Northern lineage and his descendants guided Solomon. These priestly descendants came to be called Kohanim.

Ahijah was clearly disenchanted with Solomon's priestly selections, his consolidation policies, and specifically with his international policies. His international policy was highlighted by his many marriages. Sheba was only one of his numerous wives. One of the consequences of engaging with women from other nations and bringing them to his court was they brought with them their religious traditions, idols, and deities. We can assume that at least some his marriages were also designed to cement political alliances but the text seems to imply that Solomon also just liked the ladies.

Adonijah interpreted these actions as the ultimate violation of our covenant with God. It was the primary reason for God gifting ten tribes to Jeroboam.

The text informs us that Solomon re-fortified and retained control of the northern town of Millo. When Solomon nationalized a town he assumed control of its main source of income, which in this instance was trade. Millo was near David's ancestral home and could have seriously antagonized its inhabitants as well further aggravating their resentment towards Solomon's policies. It stands to reason that the towns, villages, cities and tribes that suffered economic hardship as a result of Solomon's practices would support Jeroboam, especially since he was endorsed by a prophet.

At this juncture Jeroboam appears to be anything but the evil ruler incarnate that the text and subsequent Midrashim make him out to be. On the contrary, he is depicted as a man of character favored by God. The text further embellishes his character when it compares him to God's favorite son, David. The text seems to be implying that if Jeroboam followed God's laws, he would succeed in establishing a faithful enduring house just like David's. It also follows that if Jeroboam followed God's laws he would eventually, in some manner, become connected to the Temple in Jerusalem and become the leader of a united monarchy.

> You have been chosen by Me. Reign where you wish and you shall be King over Israel. If you heed all that I command you and walk in my ways, and do what is right in My sight keeping MY laws and commandments as

My servant David did, then I will be with you. And I will build for you a lasting dynasty as I did for David. (I Kings 11:37-39)

This sounds like the first and second paragraphs of the *shema* which are found in the book of Deuteronomy. That's because the theology and political philosophy of the Deuteronomists shaped the books of Kings and believe me, they loved David.

It shouldn't come as a surprise that the circumstances surrounding Jeroboam's designation as a ruler and future king parallel David's rise to power. Both men were brought into the fold of an existent royal court. Both receive a covenantal guarantee from prophets and both men engaged in a religious reform that cemented their authority in opposition to the royal courts.

Little is known about this period and whether or not Jeroboam did any planning prior to his ascending to a position of leadership. What is known, according to the Bible, is that as soon as he was invested as the leader he seized the moment.

He immediately fortified, in the hill country of Ephraim, and then proceeded to fortify other northern cities. After all, if you lead a significant part of a nation away from its king there are bound to be repercussions. I Kings, Chapter 12 informs us that serious repercussions from Rehoboam, Solomon's son almost occurred. We are told that upon learning of Jeroboam's being crowned king, Rehoboam mobilized his forces and prepared for a war. He gathered 180,000 warriors to fight against the House of Israel. It was only because a Prophet named Shemaiah convinced him not to attack that the war was averted.

> Thus said the Lord: You shall not set out to make war on your kinsmen the Israelites. Let every man return to his home. For this thing has been brought about by Me." (I Kings 12:24)

Jeroboam also realized he needed to address the religious needs of his people. He reasoned,

Now the kingdom may well return to the House of David. If these people still go up to offer sacrifices at the House of the Lord in Jerusalem, the heart of those people will turn back to their master King Rehoboam of Judah. They will kill me and return to Rehoboam. (I Kings 12:26-27)

What does it take to create a religion?

Remember, the Jerusalem-centered cult was just two generations old and vestiges of the earlier religious practices must still have remained in Beth El, Shiloh and other sites. Perhaps they were still being observed. Jeroboam could either reinvigorate these practices or could add a historical layer onto the practices that already existed in his newly formed country. The tradition of Aaron, the brother of Moses, fashioning the Golden Calf was most likely well known, and so we are informed that

> He had two golden calves made and placed one at Beth El and the other in Dan and he appointed priests from the ranks of the people who were not of Levite descent. (I Kings 12:28-31)

It seems to me that Jeroboam believed he was David's rightful successor. At the same time he recognized that in order to retain his sovereignty and supposedly lead the people back to God, he needed to recreate or invent a means of worship.

And this is where, according to the redactors of the Bible, that he erred. He constructed two places of worship, one at Beth El on the northern border of Judah and the other in Dan at the most northern border of his country and then he appointed priests from the people who were not of Levitical descent. And at that point, he lost God's blessing.

If the history of the Jewish people had been written by the representatives from the Northern tribes Jeroboam would be viewed as the George Washington of Israel. But the influence the authors of Deuteronomy who stressed that sacrifice could only take place in the Jerusalem Temple prevailed and the man who created a nation came to be labeled the most heinous leader in Biblical history. The man whose actions allegedly resulted in the destruction of the Northern Kingdom by the Assyrian Empire some two hundred years later.

It is interesting how politics and historical memory reflects or projects an understanding of history. Up until this point, we were told the story of a man of outstanding leadership and moral ability who, in order to succeed in his task, made specific choices. He made hard deliberate choices that any leader must make, depending upon the circumstances of the time. Choices, which when viewed through the eyes of the editors and redactors living hundreds of years later in Babylon and in Jerusalem, were considered to be reprehensible, a violation of their understanding of what Jewish life and worship should be. But was he truly as evil as he was depicted? Probably not.

The Bible records two incidents between Jeroboam and Ahijah. The first is the one where Ahijah predicts his succession. The second occurred towards the end of his life, when in Chapter 14, Jeroboam's son becomes deathly ill. According to the authors, Jeroboam understands how badly he had transgressed God's mandate and as a result was afraid to ask Ahijah for help. In desperation he sent his wife in disguise to inquire of the prophet about his future and the welfare of his son.

Ahijah was very old and according to the text was blind, however, he received a message from God, foretelling the visit along with instructions how to respond. Ahijah informed Jeroboam's wife of God's disappointment with her husband and how that will play out. She was told that the moment she returns home her son would die.

> Because I raised you up from among the people and made you a ruler over my people Israel. I tore away the Kingdom of the House of David and gave it to you. But you have not been like my servant David, who kept my commandments and followed me with all his heart, doing only what was right in my sight. You have acted worse than all those who preceded you and you have gone and made other gods for yourselves and molten images to vex me and me. You have cast me behind your back. Therefore I will

bring disaster upon the House of Jeroboam and will cut off from Jeroboam every male; I will sweep away the house as dung is swept away. Anyone belonging to Jeroboam who dies in the town shall be devoured by dogs and any one dies in the open country shall be eaten by the birds of the air. (I Kings 14:7-11)

Ahijah was quite a guy. The rabbis and the great ones who came after them thought very highly of him. Maimonides claimed he was Elijah's teacher. Some of the rabbis in the Talmud consider him to be one of the thirty-six righteous people who were necessary to keep the world from being destroyed.

But Jeroboam was also quite impressive. As maligned a character as he was made out to be in the book of Kings, he was remarkably successful. He led a bloodless rebellion and he established a religion and a country that lasted for more than two centuries. He was a leader and embodied at least initially, before the editors of the text began to subject him to their concept of what Judaism was supposed to be at that time, a person who embodied the noblest of qualities. He was destined to be a second David, one of God's favorites.

*The story of Jeroboam son of Nebat leaves us with a number of lessons. To be a leader, one must sometimes be prepared to pay a price. What we read in history, specifically religious history, may not be a reflection of the reality of the times and we have to remember it is being told through the eyes of the victors. Jeroboam's story also helps us to understand the importance of the Northern kingdom and the role and influence it played on the development of Judaism and Jewish life.*

The only personality from the time of Jeroboam until the destruction of the Temple who was referred to as being likened to David, was a man named Josiah who lived more than three centuries later. But that's another story.

# 5

# Jezebel

## NOT THE WIFE OF YOUR DREAMS

*The story of Jezebel can be found in I Kings, Chapters 16-21. It tells the story of a person of power who is governed by her personal interests. In a sense it represents the dangers which can occur when the wrong people assume power. The story of Jezebel challenges us to suppress our hostile instincts and basic desires and to learn how to respond differently.*

The most sophisticated, swanky, hip kosher restaurant in Manhattan in 2013 was a gourmet fleishig (meat) restaurant in the Soho neighborhood. The name of the restaurant was called "Jezebel", a name it was able to maintain for six months until the Orthodox Kashrut establishment forced them to change, along with a few of their policies. The religious authorities insisted that the staff dress differently, (no more sexy black leotards) and only serve wine that had been certified kosher. The owners, for better or worse, relinquished the name Jezebel and selected the less threatening term of "The J".

When I read the announcement of its opening I wondered why that name was chosen. Were they being playful or just naïve? Clearly the representatives of the religious right understood the name "Jezebel" to imply that the proprietors were stretching someone's moral code.

"Jezebel" found its way into the North American vocabulary as a result of a film made 1938 starring Bette Davis. The film was remade in 1953 and titled, *Sins of Jezebel* starring Paulette Goddard. During that period and perhaps as a result of Christian lore the name "Jezebel" came to be associated with fallen or abandoned women. Comparing a person to Jezebel suggested she was an apostate masquerading as a servant of God who manipulated and or seduced the saints of God into sins of idolatry and sexual immorality.

It was a great name for a restaurant.

The biblical character Jezebel lived approximately three decades after the Northern Kingdom seceded from Judah. Following the death of Jeroboam's son, a war of succession occurred and the victor was a general named Omri. Omri ruled for twenty-two years and was succeeded by his son Ahab. Ahab married Jezebel.

Jezebel's story begins in I Kings Chapter 16 where we learn about the exploits of her husband, Ahab. Her story is recounted in II Kings Chapter 9. When we think of Jezebel we should also think of Elijah and Elisha and the period between the 870-850 B.C.E.

Jezebel was a Phoenician princess and the daughter of the King of Tyre. She worshipped the god Baal. She and Ahab were married in order to cement a Phoenician political alliance. The alliance expanded Israel's trade routes and provided a wedge against the growing Assyrian empire. One of the alliance's stipulations permitted Jezebel to establish the worship of her God (Baal) in Ahab's court. Unfortunately, Ahab's conversion to Baal worship served as a catalyst for a grass-roots revolt led by two prophets, Elijah and Elisha. The highpoint of this story is recorded in the haftarah for *Ki Tissa* which tells of the contest between Elijah and the four hundred and fifty prophets of Baal.

There are a number of dramatic stories in the Elijah-Elisha cycle and two of them reveal Jezebel's character. I Kings, Chapter 21 informs us that a man named Naboth owned a vineyard adjacent to the King's palace and that Ahab, King of Samaria, and Jezebel's husband, desired to acquire it and transform it into a vegetable garden. He offered to purchase or trade Naboth land more suited for a vineyard than the one he presently owned.

Naboth refused.

> The Lord forbid that I should give up what I have inherited from my father's (I Kings 21:3)

Ahab returned home and began to pout. Being a good wife Jezebel told him not to worry. She would take care of it.

> Now is the time to show yourself king over Israel. Rise up and eat something, and be cheerful; I will get the vineyard of Naboth for you. (I Kings 21:7)

And she did. She wrote letters in Ahab's name to the elders and nobles of the community and arranged for thugs to testify that Naboth was an apostate and was inciting rebellion against the king. After a public humiliation, Naboth was brought to the outskirts of town and stoned to death.

Upon learning of Naboth's death, Jezebel encouraged Ahab to acquire the desired property which he immediately did.

In this instance, Jezebel is portrayed as the instigator of the theft of ancestral land. Whether or not this was the prerogative of the royalty of Tyre and therefore would be considered at least understandable is irrelevant to the story's authors who utilize this incident to demonstrate Jezebel's haughtiness and disdain for local customs.

Immediately following this incident, Elijah, who had already defeated the prophets of Baal and was constantly being pursued by Jezebel's soldiers, entered the picture.

> And the word of the Lord came to Elijah saying, Go down and meet with King Ahab in the vineyard of Naboth. Speak to him and tell him that because he has killed and illegally taken possession of the property, that in the place where the dogs licked the blood of Naboth shall the dogs lick his blood. …Because he has done evil in the eyes of the Lord I will bring evil onto him and will sweep him and every male in his house away. And for Jezebel, the dogs shall eat Jezebel by the wall of Israel. (I Kings 21:17-24)

The second incident is recorded in the II Kings Chapter 9.

Jehu, the man appointed by the prophet Elisha to rebel against the Ahab's family the Omrides, succeeds in killing Jezebel's son and son-in-law.

Jezebel's reaction is startling. One would think she would mourn, tear her clothes and cover herself with sackcloth and ashes. Not exactly.

Upon learning what has occurred, and perhaps realizing that Jehu would come for her next, she does the opposite. She dresses herself in her finest, and paints her eyes with *kohl,* an ancient mascara. She has her hair done and sits and waits for her would-be assassin to arrive while sitting in the palace balcony.

Fully prepared she waits for Jehu and as he enters the area in front of the palace she calls out to him in a disdainful manner,

> Is all well, Zimri, murderer of your master. (II Kings, 9:31)

He looks up toward the window and notices her and replies, *who is on my side, who?* Two or three palace servants described as eunuchs hear his call and lean toward him to better understand his words.

Throw her down, he said. And they picked her up and threw her from the balcony. Her blood spattered on the wall and in reaction the horses trampled her.

Jezebel is dead and Jehu, now joined by the eunuchs, went into a nearby Inn to eat and drink. After a while, Jehu reconsidered and said to his fellow men, it's not appropriate to leave that cursed woman outside. After all *for she was a king's daughter.* Go outside and claim her body and bury her.

The eunuchs followed his command *and went outside to bury her; but all they found was her skull, the feet and the hands.* The story concludes with the phrase,

This is was Jezebel. (II Kings 9:37)

Haughty, overly proud, successfully converting her husband to idolatry and willing to go to any lengths to obtain her desires- this was Jezebel. The woman whose character came to embody all that was immoral and sinful. That's why they named the restaurant in her name and that's why the rabbis of modernity forced the owners to change it. It was sinful-icious.

# 6

# Hulda the Prophet

*Hulda's story is a preface to the master story of Josiah. It challenges us to ask how we would behave when confronting impending disaster. It leads us to the understanding that religious leaders don't always hear the word of God and that hearing God's voice is not restricted to lineage or wealth. This story teaches us that leaders, true leaders, can make a difference.*

Women prophets were not unusual in ancient Judah, Israel, and the ancient Near East. Moses's sister, Miriam was called a prophet. Deborah, whose story is found in the book of Judges, is called both a judge and a prophet. The book of Nehemiah speaks of a woman prophet named Noadiah and Isaiah indicates his wife was a prophet. Unfortunately for us, her name was not recorded.

The man the Bible considers to be one of the greatest reformers was named Josiah, who ruled Judah just before the Temple and Jerusalem were destroyed in 586 B.C.E. One of the pivotal characters in his story is a woman named Huldah, a prophet.

Huldah lived in a town called Mishneh. (This should not be confused with the volumes of law which are called the Mishnah). The town of Mishneh was located on a hill immediately to the west of the city of David (Zephaniah 1:10). King Hezekiah, Josiah's great grandfather, built a wall surrounding it, in order to protect and accommodate the growing population of Jerusalem who were fleeing from the Assyrian invasion in the North.

Most of the Prophets, including Elijah and Elisha were politically active. God spoke to then through visions or voices and these visions or voices stimulated this activism. Being a prophet in those days meant when you saw an injustice you had to speak up and try to correct it. The prophets, by in large, were committed to social justice and more often than not, were critical of the excesses of kings and priests. Hulda was a different kind of prophet. She worked for the royal court and generally kept to herself. She was a union girl.

Before we meet Hulda and hear her story, we'll need a little background.

The Bible depicts Josiah's grandfather, Manasseh, as a very bad king. The author or authors of the Books of Kings considered him to be the person responsible for more sins against God than any other king. Indeed, according to the Bible, his actions were responsible for the destruction of Jerusalem. We are told that he promoted all sorts of idolatrous practices and foreign worship.

> He built altars for all the host of heaven in the two courts of the House of the Lord. He consigned his son to the fire; he practiced soothsaying and divination, and consulted with ghosts and familiar spirits. (II Kings 21:4-8).

And because of all the horrendous things he did, the Bible tells us that God would:

> Bring disaster on Jerusalem and Judah and will wipe Jerusalem clean as one wipes a dish and turns it upside down. And that God would cast off the remnant of his own people and deliver them into the hands of their enemies. (II Kings 21:11-14)

Manasseh was succeeded by his son Amon. Amon behaved just like his father and was assassinated by his courtiers within a year thus allowing his eight year old son, Josiah, to become king.

It is likely that he was governed or guided by a regent, after all, how many eight year olds would you trust to rule a kingdom?

Ultimately, Josiah turned out to be a great king and ruled for thirty-one years. During the eighteenth year of his reign, or according to some, the twelfth year, he commissioned the high priest Hilkiah to refurbish the Temple. Carpenters, masons, and workers were engaged and paid for by the crown. In the midst of the renovation, a scroll of the *Teaching of the Lord* was discovered. Hilkiah, the high priest, delivered it to the scribe Shaphan who was a member of Josiah's inner circle. And…

> When the king heard the words of the scroll of the Teaching, he rent his clothes and gave orders to the priest Hilkiah, and his scribes and ministers to inquire of the Lord on my behalf and on behalf of the people, and on behalf all of Judah, concerning the words of this scroll that has been found. For great indeed must be the wrath of the Lord that has been kindled against us, because our fathers did not obey the words of this scroll to all that has been prescribed for us. (II Kings 22:11-13).

What could this scroll have contained? It is likely that it included three portions from the middle of the Book of Deuteronomy. (Chapters 11-26). That is to say, the Torah portions which begin with the blessings and the curses (*Re-eh*) are followed by Judges (*Shoftim*), and conclude with When you go out (*Ki tetze*).

Imagine! Josiah heard these chapters and learned that his people were going to be the recipients of colossal curses, their Temple would be destroyed, their government crushed and all the people exiled from their land. No wonder he puts on sackcloth and ashes and tears his garments as a sign of mourning.

Sometime after the immediate shock wore off, Josiah ordered the High Priest to lead a delegation of scribes and ministers to the only person who could possibly help to avert the severe decree. Hulda, the prophet.

This is very interesting because wouldn't you think Josiah should have asked the High Priest to intervene directly with God to change the evil decree? Wasn't it the High Priest who enters the Holy of Holies every Yom Kippur and prays for forgiveness on our behalf?

This simple act was extremely revealing. Priests trace their legitimacy back to the children of Aaron. People are priests as a result of their blood lines, their lineage. They performed specific actions in specific places. They took care of the Ark and once it was built, the Temple. Asking God for advice just might not have been part of their job description.

Prophets, on the other hand, simply happen. They could be anyone and they could live anywhere. They could be shepherds like Amos, or Levitical Priests like Jeremiah. Biblical prophets prophesied in and outside of Israel. If you remember Jonah, was sent to Nineveh. Nineveh was a major city in the Assyrian Empire which now is modern day Iraq.

Let's examine what Hulda said:

> So the priest Hilkiah, and Ahikam, Achbor, Shaphan and Asaiah went to the prophetess Huldah, -the wife of Shallum -.the keeper of the wardrobe- who was living in Jerusalem in the Mishneh, and they spoke to her. (II Kings 22:14)

What would they have asked? "Hulda, we found this scroll in the Temple and it has convinced the king that we have really gone astray and bad things, real bad things are going to happen to all of us. The king is in a panic and we are beginning to worry about him. He has begun to mourn for the entire kingdom. He's wearing sackcloth and has poured ashes over his head. What should we do?"

Or,

"Hulda, we found this scroll that says we really messed up and God is going to punish us, like he punished the Egyptians. Is there anything you can do?"

> She responded:"Thus said the Lord, the God of Israel: Say to the man who sent you to me: Thus said the Lord: I am going to bring disaster upon this place and its inhabitants, in accordance with all the words of the scroll which the king of Judah has read. Because they have forsaken Me and have made offerings to other gods and vexed Me with all their deeds, My wrath is kindled against this place and it shall not be quenched, But say to this the king of Judah, who sent you to inquire of the Lord: Thus said the Lord the God of Israel: As for the words which you have heard-because your heart was softened and you humbled yourself before the Lord when you heard what I decreed against this place and its inhabitants- that it will become a desolation and a curse-and because you rent your clothes and wept before Me, I for my part have listened-declares the Lord. Assuredly, I will gather you to your fathers and you will be laid in your tomb in peace. Your eyes shall not see all the disaster which I will bring upon this place. (II Kings 22:15-21).

Huldah tells the delegation Josiah is correct. Judah (Jerusalem) is going to be destroyed. But because Josiah repented, and supposedly is going to institute big changes, the destruction will be postponed until after his death. And, because of the way Josiah responded to the finding of this scroll, his death will be a peaceful one, meaning he will be buried with his ancestors the kings of Judah. Being buried with your family was a big thing then just like it is now.

But once he dies destruction will follow. The Reforms began around 621 B.C.E. Twenty four years later (597 B.C.E.) Jerusalem was conquered and the first exile to Babylon occurred. Eleven years after that Jerusalem was sacked and the Temple destroyed.

The story of how Josiah instituted his reforms and transformed the country is remarkable and the incident told about a woman prophet raises some interesting questions. Hulda's prophecy provided Josiah with a call to action. *Perhaps one of the hidden lessons in the story is that having a purpose a sense of mission provides each of us with the opportunity to change.*

The royal delegation's field trip to Hulda demonstrated the limits or possible weakness of the priesthood. God did not speak to the High Priest. Lineage doesn't ensure holiness.

Hulda informs us that exile and destruction will occur as a result of Josiah's grandfather, Manasseh's behavior. It may be difficult to absorb this, but it suggests we are responsible for the sins and transgressions of our fathers. The statement was most likely added to the story at a later time by people who had a different political agenda; but as it stands, it seems to imply that we have the ability, if we try, to change our behavior. All of us inherit some of the attitudes and behaviors of our parents and grandparents but we don't have to have as they did. If we try, we can become the type of person we want to be.

*Hulda's story challenges us on two levels. Initially it appears that if she listened to her inner voice, the voice that the text claims is God's voice, she could be risking treason. After all, consider what would happen if someone, in front of witnesses, predicted the death of a President? It must have taken the courage of her convictions for her to address the King. Leaders must be willing to listen to their inner voices and to take risks. Josiah also demonstrated one of the necessary qualities of a good leader. He listened. He heard Hulda's words, her sincerity, and was willing to alter the course of his rule. Good leaders, great leaders, need to be able to both articulate their vision and to hear the wisdom in others.*

# 7

# Josiah

## THE GRAND REORGANIZATION

*Josiah's story suggests a number of different lessons which we can learn. Since his father, Amon, reigned for only two years prior to being assassinated, we can assume he didn't teach Josiah how to be a leader. On the other hand he might have learned a great deal from his grandfather, Manasseh (whose story follows this one). This, of course challenges you, the reader, to think about their lives and their leadership abilities in the context of the world in which they lived. Ask yourselves: What are Josiah's dominant character traits? What skills were required to achieve his goals? And finally, what are the lessons I can learn from his story?*

Josiah is the most important leader in the Bible you've never heard of.

Let's face it, there are leaders and there are leaders. Some people are placed into positions of leadership and others rise to the occasion. Great leadership is the ability to cause a fundamental shift in the way cultures or societies operate. Moses is clearly the most important leader in the bible. Moses gathered together a mixed multitude of peoples lead them out of servitude and shaped them into a nation. We need not say more.

Joshua continued in his footsteps, and ranks second in importance as a biblical leader. He brought a people into a new land, theoretically conquered it, (though today we know that the conquest was less of a conquest and more of a gradual settlement), divided it among the tribes and, like his predecessor, led them in a ceremony of swearing allegiance to the Covenant. Several institutions and ceremonies have their origins in the book of Joshua. The institution of the Passover sacrifice and circumcision parallel the entry to the land. Joshua was also responsible for transporting the Ark of the Covenant which eventually becomes the repository for the Torah. He successfully shifted and transformed the culture, the society of the descendants who had left Egypt.

But Josiah comes in next, even before the prophet and kingmaker Samuel, or Moses' brother Aaron, the leader of the priests. Josiah was a great leader and a great king who lived just a few decades before the Babylonian conquest of Jerusalem and the rest of the kingdom of Judah beginning in 597 B.C.E.

As the first king, David expanded the borders of Israel and established Jerusalem as the political and religious center of his government. He was at least initially a successful leader but as he aged he lost his momentum, became involved in a tawdry affair and several of his sons rebelled against him. It almost seems that his deficits cancelled out his successes. Solomon succeeded him and built the Temple and in doing so nearly bankrupted the country. Again a major accomplishments but it didn't result in major societal shifts.

It is true that David's (1005-965 B.C.E.) centralization and Solomon's (968-928) building projects represent the high points of the Israelite, Judean monarchy. However, if one looks at what happened in Judean history from those points forward, one could say that from the time of the establishment of the monarchy until Josiah became King of Judah, the history of Judah and Israel consisted of constant fighting and bickering between numerous kingdoms occasionally highlighted by a few decades of peace and prosperity.

To say it another way, from the time of Solomon's building the Temple until the time of Josiah, approximately 384 years, Judean society was static, lacking any societal innovation.

Josiah was eight years old when he became king and his long and successful reign was responsible for a fundamental shift in the society of his time. The Bible considers him to be the ideal monarch. II Kings, Chapter 22 compares him to David but adds the phrase, *and he did not turn from the right or the left*. This is important because it was only used in the Bible when referring to Moses and Joshua. The text also states that there

> …was no king like Josiah who returned to YHWH with all his heart and with all his soul and with all his power according to the Torah of Moses. (II Kings 23:25).

Josiah's great-grandfather also attempted to change the structure of the government. Hezekiah ruled Judah (Jerusalem) at a time when the neighboring countries of Syria and Egypt tried to force Judah into an alliance in order to defend themselves against the encroaching Assyrian empire. They threatened to invade and conquer Judah if Hezekiah refused. In an attempt to ward off any attack, Hezekiah attempted to re-position and re-organize his country. Some his innovations were not successful and didn't achieve completion until his great-grandson became king. But he was able to reinforce the walls of Jerusalem and dig a water tunnel in order to ensure a water supply in case the attack occurred (That tunnel exists to this day, known as Hezekiah's tunnel).

In desperation Hezekiah sought protection from Sennacherib (705-681), then the Emperor of Assyria. (II Kings 18:13-19:37) records this incident and describe the tribute that Hezekiah was forced to pay in order to become an Assyrian vassal.

Sixty years later the tapestry of the ancient world had once again changed. The Assyrian Empire's influence and might was in eclipse. After Assurbanipal, the last great ruler of Assyria, died in 627 B.C.E., the revolt began against

Assyria led by the founder of the Neo-Babylonian Empire. This change in the international scene coincided with Josiah's becoming King.

There are two different versions that describe Josiah's reign. One of them is found in the second book of Kings, the other is in the second book of Chronicles. Chronicles is the younger of the two sources, perhaps compiled in the early fourth century B.C.E. The older source, II Kings, explains that Josiah became King when he was eight years old and when he became eighteen he authorized a refurbishing of the Temple. Apparently during the Temple clean up a *Scroll of the Teaching of the House of the Lord* was discovered. It is unclear who was actually responsible for the writing of this scroll (it's a chicken and egg scenario) but on the basis of the content that was in the scroll, Josiah reorganized Judean life. He peacefully expanded the borders of Judah to approximately what it was before the country had split into two countries under Solomon's son, Rehoboam (928 B.C.E.), and he created a new form religious life that paved the way for what today is referred to as Judaism.

What did Josiah do?

In order to understand his accomplishments you need to imagine a country as a business, a relatively large business. Josiah somehow realized that the business he was supposed to run, which was a hereditary business, wasn't working. It was not only in danger of being bought up by a larger business, the Babylonian Empire, but it was also constantly being attacked by the medium size corporations of Egypt and Syria.

In order to protect his interests and his investors, the people of his kingdom, he reorganized everything. First, he centralized. At that time, justice was being delivered by the elders who lived in each little town or city. Josiah replaced them with trained priests, who knew how to read and write and could follow the laws he had either written or inherited.

Many of these priests used to live in used to be called the Kingdom of Israel. Not the Israel we think of today, just the Northern part. These priests who lived in places like Beth El, Shechem and perhaps Tiberius, had all fled when the Assyrians attacked and conquered Israel some sixty or so years earlier. It is likely that Josiah negotiated with the Jerusalem priesthood and created positions for these Northern priests. In return for a concession that they wouldn't have an equal place in the Temple, he put them in charge of the local elders.

In addition, he insisted that all sacrifices take place centrally, in the Temple in Jerusalem. This was a huge undertaking but with the civil servants for whom he had just created jobs and who we are going to call Levites, in place, he was able to make this happen.

Imagine how difficult it was for the people to make this religious shift. All of a sudden they couldn't worship and pray to God the way they had been worshipping and praying to for generations. In response to this shift to a central place of worship people began to gather in their homes or in public places and pray. This was one of the ways that what today we call synagogues developed.

Finally, Josiah created a national holiday. Well he didn't just create it. Joshua, Moses' successor had celebrated it hundreds of years earlier. At that time Joshua assembled the people and offered a sacrifice and at a subsequent festival baked and ate unleavened bread, matzah. Josiah combined this festival with a festival of freedom and incorporated the telling of the story of the Exodus.

Yes, he created the basis for our celebration of Passover.

Remarkable, no? Josiah just didn't wake up and say, I am going to reorganize the life of my people. Things don't work that way. Reorganization on this scale takes major planning, sometimes years of planning.

1. He assembled and established a new covenant with the people.

2. He centralized the monarchy and declared that sacrifice (worship) could only take place in Jerusalem. In order for this to be accomplished it was necessary to remove all objects that represented

foreign deities from the Temple as well as destroy any religious sites dedicated to other deities throughout Judah and where possible Israel. This included destroying the sanctuary at Beth El, burning any vessels which were used for idolatrous purposes throughout the country. It also included removing any signs of Canaanite gods or goddesses, and abolishing cult prostitution.

3. He commandeered the priests from the North and empowered them to oversee the current judicial system which was governed by local tribal elders. We underestimate the value and the influence these priests had on the development of Jewish life. Let's call them Levites.

4. He combined a festival of freedom with a festival of unleavened bread into what became the basis for our current Passover festival. The Bible informs us that this was the first time that Passover had been observed since the time of Joshua at Gilgal.

5. Finally, he was responsible for re-directing the search for religious inspiration and worship away from the sacrificial system without having it abolished. Josiah was responsible for creating a comprehensive document that explained, through the words of God's servant Moses, the how a people should conduct themselves.

Josiah did not conceive of the book as a substitute for Temple worship. He replaced the system of worship which was based on a system that posited a divinely ordained king with a book that served as the basis for future revelation and in doing so elevated the book to the level of a significant religious object. This created the foundations for the religion of the Book - the study of Torah.

*The Scroll of the Teaching of the House of the Lord* was most likely three portions from the middle of the Book of Deuteronomy (Chapters 11-26). That is to say, the Torah portions which begins with Re-eh (the blessings and the curses) and are followed by Shoftim (judges), and which concludes with Ki tetze ("when you go out"). Reading Deuteronomy with this in mind, you will quickly realize that the first sentence of parshat Shoftim (judges) is part of the reorganization and the constant repetition of the phrase which ends *in your gates* is because that was the place where the Levites served as judges.

> You shall appoint magistrates and officials for your tribes in all the settlements that the Lord God has given you… (Deut. 16:19)

When you read both versions of the Josiah story, two other things become apparent. First, the story is introduced by a prophet named Hulda, whose story we just read. But when you compare both versions in II Kings and II Chronicles, you notice that in one version Josiah dies in battle honoring his liege in Babylon, and in the other he is promised that as a result of his piety he would be granted the blessing of being buried with his ancestors.

Josiah was a true leader. He transformed Judean society as did Joshua and Moses before him. His story teaches us about leadership and that people have the ability to not only change their destiny but the destiny of those who surround them.

*Josiah was a great leader whose story teaches us that change requires thoughtful planning, that opportunities for change exist if we just take the time to look at things differently, and that if we wish to change ourselves or our families, or our businesses, we have to believe it can be accomplished. One of the pivotal characters in his story is a woman named Hulda, a prophet.*

# 8

# Manasseh the Conundrum

## WHEN BAD THINGS HAPPEN TO GOOD PEOPLE

*Manasseh is one of the most maligned characters in the Bible. According to traditional interpretation, Haman was bad; Manasseh was worse. Yet he ruled Israel for fifty-five years and under his guidance the nation did not enter into a war. It emerged as a secure, prosperous peaceful country. He must have done something right. Ask yourself, "what did he do and what lessons can be learned if we place the text in its proper historical context and remover the authors' biases"?*

Here is his story as if they were in his own words…..

I've been having visions as of late. Is it because my death is near? Is this something that happens to people when they approach the nadir of their lives? I'm hesitant to speak about it to others- it might hasten my demise. The visions are connected to a book called "The Bible" that is somehow connected to both my ancestors and descendants. I travel the length and breadth of that book, back and forth, up and down, forward and backward seemingly at random. I arrive at certain junctures and words and stories fill my head and then suddenly, I am back in my home in Jerusalem.

These visions are providing me with an understanding, assuming what I am seeing or reading is entirely correct, of the role I played in the development of the Jewish people. Whoever put that book together really didn't like me. I am not nor ever was the person they described me to be. What did I do to cause such enmity?

Let me just give you a sample of their distaste: There is story towards the end of a book called Judges, Chapter 18 to be exact; a story which predates my family line, about the tribe of Dan who, while searching for new lands to conquer, came upon a man named Micah and his family who employed a Levite, a priest, to minister to his household.

Micah had constructed some sort of a sanctuary in which he had placed a molten image and an ephod and some *teraphim*. *Teraphim* were little statues of the household spirits. The Dan tribe desired to have their own priest and wanted the priest that was serving Micah's household as their own. They intimidated Micah - well they actually threatened to kill him - if he didn't relinquish the priest. The priest clearly perceived the opportunity to serve a tribe instead of a single family as a promotion and willingly took the job.

We are told the priest's name was Jonathan, the son of Gershom, the son of …. And this is where it gets tricky. Gershom's father's name is written in an unusual manner. The letters *Mem*, *Shin*, *Heh*, or Moshe, (Moses), were written in normal size, but between the *mem* and the *shin*, a small *nun* was inserted which changed the name from Moses to Manasseh, my name.

The text originally explained that Jonathan was the grandson of Moses but the editors of the text changed his name to mine. Why would they do that?

Perhaps because they didn't want to empower the Levites, Moses' descendants, in the Temples outside of Jerusalem. Perhaps these priests, let's call them Kohanim, desired worship to be centralized and to take place in one place, the holy city of Jerusalem. Perhaps they added that extra letter in order to identify that priest with me because they detested the religious policies I followed when I was King of Judah and they desired to discredit the grandson of Moses!

I'm getting ahead of myself.

My name is Manasseh, I was twelve years old when I became King. Thank the Lord that my father, Hezekiah guided me and served as my regent for a decade. One needs to learn how to be a good King and my father was, at least he tried to be a good king. He became king around 727 and died around 698. Not a bad run for a king. Twenty-nine years.

One often asks, "What makes a good king?" Does one become known as a good king simply because he was a just person? Consider, for example David my ancient ancestor, would he have been considered a good king? I think that David, at times, and during certain periods of his rule, was a very popular king. He also was the first king to have a chronicler on staff and believe me that helps get the word out. But was he good king?

David had a dark side. He was a philanderer. He played the northern tribes against those in the south and he failed to institute succession planning which was one of the reasons why his sons were constantly revolting. He consistently abandoned his friends for personal gain. Uriah the Hittite, one of his original followers was discarded when David developed the hots for his wife Bat Sheba. Uriah's uncle Joab, constantly placed David's and the nation's needs over his own. He lasted a little longer but ultimately perished by David's command. David swore never to raise a hand against King Saul, but when he was king he systematically eradicated Saul's descendants and in a manner that theoretically freed him from blame until Rizpah, Saul's concubine, created a national incident. What kind of king was he and how could we describe David's style of leadership? It's complicated.

What about David's son, Solomon, was he a good king? What type of leader was he? Well great ancestor Solomon is certainly well known. He allegedly was gifted with wisdom. Again, there is nothing better than good press and believe me I have a lot more to say about that later. Yes, he built the Temple but in doing so, he bankrupted the entire country. As a matter of fact he put us into so much debt that he was forced to cede towns and cities to Hiram the king of Tyre in order to pay his bills.

He did establish Jerusalem as an international center, but if one studies history, one learns that Jerusalem's so called prominence in the international community was more of a creative fiction than sophisticated proactive policy. Solomon might have built the Temple but he was also responsible for the introduction of other forms of worship in Judah and Israel. His plethora of wives brought with them their own priests and religious traditions. In less than a generation Israel went from a monotheistic nation to one that embraced an ancient form of pluralism.

The so called alliances he made that are recorded in the Bible were temporary at best and fell apart almost immediately following his death. Oh, yes, great ancestor Solomon was never the regent my father was. Within a short time after his death, his son Rehoboam, who most likely had little, if any, training became King. He mishandled the tribes so badly that a rebellion occurred and the country split into two. If it weren't for the presence of a local prophet, Judah would have gone to war with Israel. A great king? Certainly the rabbis living hundreds of years later thought so, but I doubt it.

My father was a good king. He reigned in Judah for twenty-nine years. During that time he attempted to restructure the government. I think the world was much more complicated during his early kingship than it is today. The Assyrians were in the process of establishing an empire. They accomplished this as a result of a technologically sophisticated army which was able to rapidly advance. They quickly conquered a series of smaller kingdoms and incorporated their territories into their empire as provinces. They deported the elite of these populations and settled them in other regions thus destroying their national identities and at the same time eliminating the future threat of rebellion. Damascus fell in 732 B.C.E. and Samaria (the northern kingdom) ten years later in the sixth year of my father's reign. Egypt and some of the neighboring countries formed an alliance hoping to stop the Assyrian aggression and remain independent. They approached my father and threatened to attack Judah if he refused to ally with them.

The prophet Isaiah counseled my father against this alliance with Egypt. My father ignored this advice and joined the alliance. In the meantime, city by city, forty-six cities were conquered on the Assyrians' march to Jerusalem.

In an attempt to prepare for the siege my father attempted to transform the government. The Bible records his story from a religious perspective, (we will address the world of Biblical politics later on), but believe me there was an underlying strategy. The books of Kings and Chronicles explain his actions stemmed from his personal and religious beliefs and so they claim that's why he abolished the cults of the high places, smashed the copper serpent which Moses made in the desert, and concentrated religious activity in the Jerusalem Temple.

It was his intent to raise the status of the Jerusalem Temple as the only legitimate form of worship in Judah because it promoted national unity and would strengthen the ties between the people of Judah and the Davidic dynasty. The book of Chronicles informs us that he sent letters to the remnants of the tribes in the North, Manasseh and Ephraim and invited them to offer the sacrificial Paschal Lamb in the Temple during Passover. Just another act to further bolster national unity.

The Assyrian advance began in 712 B.C.E. My Father, anticipating war, began to stockpile and store grains, oil and wine. He fortified the provincial towns and in order to assure that Jerusalem had a more than adequate water supply he diverted the spring waters of Gihon through a tunnel to the pool of Siloam. Neighboring countries, including Egypt sought an alliance. They more or less coerced my father into joining them and promised military support which never really arrived. The Assyrian army continued to advance and as the troops were surrounding the city my father surrendered. Jerusalem became an Assyrian's province. My father paid heavy tribute but Judah survived.

When my father died in 705 B.C.E., I became king of the province of Judah in the Empire of Assyria. I served the Assyrian Emperors well, all of them - Sennacherib, Esarhaddon, and Sargon. I had a country to rebuild. I did what I was told.

It was a little easier for me than it was for my predecessors. I was the first king who didn't have to be concerned about the rival kingdom of Israel since it had been destroyed fifteen years earlier and a significant portion of its population had been deported. I supported my Assyrian overloads and even led what remained of my army into Egypt at their command.

What I really did and was to bring fifty-five years of peace to a troubled land. I revived Judah's rural economy and achieved a most favored nation status with Assyria. By restoring rural worship I established strong ties with the local aristocracy and was able to stimulate the economy. It's true I was forced to undo most of what my father had achieved, but in return I was able to attain similar goals and then again, I didn't have much of a choice. And, I brought peace and prosperity to my people.

If the Assyrians, my masters, wished to build temples to their deities I permitted it. If the locals wished to return to their prior forms of local worship I allowed it. In return they planted what I requested, paid their taxes, allowed me to build the roads I desired. I increased our ability to produce and export olives, olive oil and fruits. Trade increased and the people prospered. It was a quid pro quo. The population in the Beersheba valley and in the highlands grew, towns and cities were rebuilt. Ekron and Gaza were reconstructed and the forts in Arad and Usa were rebuilt in order to protect the trade routes. Under my guidance, Judah experienced the longest period of peace and prosperity in its history. I was, I am a good and just ruler.

But the priests who lived after my death, the ones who supported Josiah and later on in Babylon helped to construct the Bible, despised me. All that I had accomplished was meaningless to them because it conflicted with their agenda. One would think that bringing peace and prosperity to a people would be admired, but no, those who redacted the Bible and the rabbis who followed hundreds of years later viewed my successes as obstructions to their goals. What kind of man did they think I was? I know what kind of a man they thought I was; just read what they wrote about me:

> He did what was displeasing to the Lord, following the abhorrent practices of the nations that the Lord had dispossessed before the Israelites. He rebuilt shrines that his father Hezekiah had destroyed; he erected altars for Baal. He bowed down to all the host of heaven and worshiped them and he built altars for them in the House of the Lord.
>
> He consigned his son to fire; he practiced soothsaying and divination and consulted ghosts and familiar spirits. And Manasseh led them astray to do greater evil than the nations that the Lord had destroyed before the Israelites. Therefore the Lord spoke through his prophets and said,
>
> Because King Manasseh of Judah has done these abhorrent things-he has outdone in wickedness all that the Amorites did before his time-and because he led Judah to sin with his fetishes, I am going to bring such a disaster on Jerusalem and Judah that both ears of everyone who hears about it will tingle. I will wipe Jerusalem clean as one wipes a dish and turns it upside down. I will cast off the remnant of My own people and deliver them into the hands of their enemies. They shall be plunder and prey to all their enemies.
>
> Moreover Manasseh put so many innocent people to death that he filled Jerusalem with blood from end to end (II Kings 21:1-16)

They even denied me a place in the world to come and equated my actions akin to those of Haman. They created legends that my mother was the prophet Isaiah's daughter and that I judged him and condemned him to death. Really!

Apparently those who put the Bible into writing weren't united in their disdain. Those who wrote the books of Kings abhorred me. I really think they were Jerusalem Priests. Those who wrote the books of Chronicles were somewhat gentler. They were unable to reconcile my long reign with the wickedness that was reported in my name. After all I lived longer than any other monarch and died peacefully and was buried in the palace garden. They also couldn't accept that my sins would be visited upon future generations. Chronicles accused me of committing religious infamy but refrained from accusing me of executing innocents. Yet both sources, both groups of people held me responsible for the destruction of Jerusalem and the exile to Babylon.

Travelling forward and backward in Biblical time has provided me with a way of understanding my ancestors' actions. Those who lived in Babylon were trying to create a platform to reinvigorate a captured, conquered people and instill them with a desire to return to their homeland. This, in their eyes, required a central and uniform place of worship, and one, that included them in a prominent position of authority. Peace lost to politics.

Yet I wonder, if in spite of the way I have been historically maligned, those of you read my story might come away with something that offers personal value. It really doesn't matter how history or one's contemporaries view you if you are dedicated and true to yourself. I brought peace and joy and prosperity to a people. History might have recorded it differently but I have no regrets. And neither should you.

*Manasseh the son of Hezekiah was King of Judah for fifty-five years. His reign can be described as the longest, most prosperous, most peaceful period in first Temple times. What was his secret? Was it worth it to submit to a greater power in order to achieve broader goals? Have you been in similar situations? Manasseh reigned from 687-642 B.C.E. How would you describe his leadership style?*

# 9

# Ezra and Nehemiah

## WHERE CAN HOLINESS BE FOUND?
## WHAT TYPE OF LEADER IS MORE EFFECTIVE?

*I live in Manhattan and hopefully will witness the completion of the first stage of the building of the Second Avenue Subway in my lifetime. The idea for this new subway line originated more than fifty years ago. The project began several times but was halted time after time for lack of funds. Huge empty tunnels stood unused below the streets of Manhattan for decades. The first stage of this project should be completed in 2015. I find it remarkable that the project has moved forward after an absence of so many years. It is a tribute to the vision of a few individuals and their leadership abilities. And this is just a subway line. Imagine how more difficult it was to build a Temple!*

*The process that transpired in order for the Temple to be rebuilt should be considered a testimony to our ancestors' on-going commitment and dedication. It should also serve as a reminder to us that hopes and dreams can be realized.*

The books of Ezra and Nehemiah directly precede Chronicles I and II which are the last two books in the Hebrew Bible. They begin where Chronicles end, and contain historical traditions, records of significant liturgical developments and preserve important genealogical lists of returnees, priests, Levites, Temple and secular leaders and personnel. They are concerned with the process leading up to the rebuilding of the Second Temple and the re-establishment of Jewish life in Israel. That it took nearly one hundred years suggests that it wasn't an easy task and that there are lessons to be learned.

This review of Ezra and Nehemiah will attempt to achieve three goals:

First, it introduces two important personalities in our tradition that are rarely mentioned.

Second, it reveals two different versions of the same story and asks us to consider how two different men wielded political authority. Success can be credited to each but focus on the qualities and characteristics of Ezra and Nehemiah that caused each of them to perform so differently even though they were mostly in similar situations.

Finally, it presents an ancient dilemma that remains ever-present. It challenges us to consider what the core value of Jewish life is. Is it ritual adherence or something else? And, what should that mean for us?

When the Temple and Jerusalem were destroyed in 586 B.C.E. the remaining Judean aristocracy, scholars, priests and craftspeople who had not left thirteen years earlier, were physically exiled and settled in Babylon. It must have been difficult for them to adjust to a new land, much like it was for many of our grandparents and great grandparents when they arrived in North America. Like our recent ancestors, the exiles from Israel assimilated into the larger more sophisticated Babylonian culture and prospered in the most urban sophisticated society in the world at that time.

They adopted Babylonian names, like Mordecai and Esther and modified their calendar so it coincided with the Babylonian calendar. The original names for the months in the Hebrew calendar were numerical; first month, second month, and so on. In Babylon the names were changed to Kislev, Tishrei, Av, you get the drift.

At the same time our ancestors became more insular. For example they lived together and began to hold community meals on the Sabbath and they began to compile the different religious traditions that were being practiced and to discuss the nature of past worship during First Temple times. This process continued in the centuries that followed in what we today call the land of Israel.

Why did I use the phrase, "what we refer to today as the land of Israel?" Because for nearly two hundred years after the death of King Solomon, what we today refer to as "Israel" was actually two countries, one in the North called "Israel" and one in the South which centered in Jerusalem and was called "Judah". Ironic isn't it? What we call Jerusalem today wasn't in Israel, it was in Judah.

This changed in 721 B.C.E. when the Northern part of the country, Israel, was destroyed by the Assyrian Empire. We assume that many of the survivors, that is to say, the priests, nobles and scholars, migrated across the border and settled in Judah. We can also assume they brought their religious and cultural traditions with them.

One hundred years later the second book Kings and the second book of Chronicles record the story of a King Josiah of Judah (Jerusalem) whose priests, according to these texts, discovered a scroll of the Lord in the Temple while undertaking the first Temple renovation in quite a long time. This book, this scroll resulted in a complete re-organization of the country. The scroll was most likely Chapters 11-26 of what today we call "Deuteronomy." The remainder of that book was added at a later time or times, most likely by the exiles that lived in Babylon.

In 538 B.C.E. the ruling Babylonian dynasty was usurped by Cyrus II (539-530) the king of Persia and Medea. One of his first acts as Emperor was one designed to demonstrate religious tolerance. Cyrus permitted subjected nations to re-establish their own temples in their native lands.

As a result of this proclamation some Judean exiles returned to Israel. These pilgrims (*olim* in Hebrew) began the process of rebuilding the Temple and resettling in Judah and its surrounding environs. Of course not everyone wished to return to the homeland, since life was very good for many of them in Babylon. Cyrus, desiring to strengthen his presence abroad, offered our ancestors financial incentives to make that long journey back to the Promised Land. Our ancestors living in Babylon, who were synthesizing and compiling our traditions into written form, considered Cyrus's actions to be the hand of God working through history.

Ezekiel and the people who we refer to as the authors of 3rd and 4th Isaiah lived in Babylon during this period and most likely assisted the exiles in 586 B.C.E. to settle and acculturate. They attempted, through their words, to inspire the exiled men and women with the hope that a return to their promised land would occur. Isaiah offered the people a vision of universal cooperation. Ezekiel suggested a national vision guided by a rejuvenated priestly class.

The first wave of the returnees left Babylon in 539 B.C.E. They were led by Sheshbazzar, a son of the Judean, King Jehoichin who was exiled to Babylon in 597 B.C.E. He was succeeded by Jehoichin's grandson, Zerubbabel. Zerubbabel means the "seed of Babel."

It appears that the first phase of the resettlement involved reconstructing the altar and reinstituting the sacrificial system. This was followed by laying the foundation for the Temple.

Like the Second Avenue subway, the work began and for a variety of political reasons stopped. Time passed and work once again commenced. Neighboring villages and cities needed to be convinced that the rebuilding of the Temple wouldn't impinge or threaten their ways of living.

Even in the earliest stages of rebuilding, grave conflicts developed between the "people of the land" and the returnees. The people of the land considered the returnees to be co-religionists,

...for we seek your God, as do you; and we sacrifice unto him since the days when you were exiled. (Ezra 4:2)

Zerubabel and the other leaders didn't think so, *You have nothing to do with us to build a house to our God;* to paraphrase the next line, *"we will do it ourselves!"*

This was the period of two of our last three prophets, Haggai and Zechariah. The third and final Jewish prophet, Malachi, lived and prophesied after the Temple had been rebuilt. Many believed that as a result of Haggai and Zechariah's efforts the work stoppage ended and construction was able to continue. It is the year 516. B.C.E. and the new Temple, what we refer to as the Second Temple, is dedicated.

We really don't know very much about what occurred in the fifty years which followed the Temple's re-establishment but we do know that in 460 B.C.E, an alliance was formed between Egypt and the newly created Delian (Athenian Greece) league. They revolted against the Babylonian empire and in order to further secure the provinces Xerxes (486-465 B.C.E.) and his son Artaxerxes (465-434 B.C.E.) who ruled in Babylon authorized a priest and a scribe named Ezra to lead another wave of immigration to the province of Judah which was now called *Yehud*. It is 458 B.C.E.

Ezra arrived in Jerusalem with a lot of clout. He was authorized by the emperor to appoint judges and to judge in accordance with the "law of the God of heaven". He also received funds from the royal treasury to reinstitute in the Temple of God of Heaven in Jerusalem sacrifices for the well-being of the king and his family. The text informs us that 1,500 people who accompanied him including priests, Levites, musicians and bureaucrats, arrived in *Yehud* with huge tax exemptions.

That is why Ezra is credited with bringing the Torah to Jerusalem.

Ezra looked around, observed how the people lived and didn't like what he saw. The descendants of those who remained and were not exiled one hundred and fifty years earlier had married the locals. They had "diluted the Jewish blood". Blood was very important to Ezra and his ancestors who had been living in Babylon because only someone who was a priest, a Kohen, could offer sacrifice in the Temple and observing and maintaining the sacrificial system (which was outlined in the Torah) was crucial to the way the priests understood their role and relationship to God. They could have reasoned, if impure priests offer sacrifices to God, God will know and won't find the offerings pleasing. He might even become angry and punish our people like he did when he exiled us.

Ezra attempted to re-establish the priesthood and to purify the Jewish people. Ezra was a tribal Jew. He, unlike others of his time and our time, considered a person to be Jewish only by virtue of his or her direct lineage.

Ezra had an agenda. He desired to separate the returnees in Judah from those who had not experienced the exile. Up until this point the phrase *am ha-aretz* (people of the land) was a positive statement reflecting the sovereignty of the locals. Ezra transformed it into a negative expression, one that continues to this day. Today *am ha-aretz* is a derogatory term that implies that people are common and ignorant of the law, a reflection of what Ezra saw upon his return.

The people initially loved him and were overwhelmed with joy because he brought the Torah and created a community wide Torah dedication. Of course he also arrived with soldiers, just in case the people didn't receive him in the manner he anticipated.

Unfortunately, it was a brief honeymoon. The people were not pleased with his initial reforms and legislative acts. They actually complained in writing to the Emperor in Babylon when he tried to force the men to divorce their non-Jewish wives.

The people became enraged and wrote to the Emperor and complained. It should come as no surprise that since many of them were extremely wealthy and paid a lot of taxes, the Emperor responded quickly and chastised Ezra, telling him to abandon his ideas of separating one people into two.

The rabbis living during Roman times some five-six hundred years later loved Ezra. Ezra, the bringer of the Law, was considered to be a second Moses. According to rabbinic legend, in addition to bring the Torah from Babylon to Jerusalem he is credited with instituting the days, the number of people and the number of verses that should be read from the Torah. And in the book of Nehemiah (8:1-9), there is a description of how Ezra assembled all of the people in Jerusalem and surrounding areas to the Temple and on the first day of the seventh month they observed Rosh Hashanah. Wow!

One would think that a person as important as Ezra would be more visible in our tradition. Yet one could sit in synagogue week after week, year after year and never read or hear of his name mentioned. I can think of a few spotty references to him on Yom Kippur but even in those instances it's without the recognition one thinks he should receive.

It was around this time that many scholars claim that another book was published, perhaps one to counter the harsh tone of Ezra. This book told the story of a non-Jewish woman, a product of marriages forbidden in the Torah on both sides of the family. She became Jewish and her descendant ended up becoming one of the great Kings of Israel. His name was David, her name was Ruth. It is 458 B.C.E.

Ezra's agenda was in danger of failing. He needed help. The Jerusalemites began to restore the city walls in order to protect themselves from other potential threats; and the ruler of Samaria, what used to be called the Northern Kingdom, fearing for his people's safety, wrote to the Emperor and claimed that if the city of Jerusalem was fully restored and its walls were completed, the revenues to the crown would diminish, since the Jerusalemites had been rebellious from time immemorial and if the walls were fully restored and the Jerusalemites could defend themselves, they would most likely either seek to conquer neighboring countries or to rebel against the Empire.

The Emperor of Babylon replaced Ezra with Nehemiah, an official of the highest rank in the court, as the new governor of Judah and agreed to the

Samarian request to halt the construction. Nehemiah served as a successful governor for several decades. Under his guidance peace and prosperity ruled. He returned to Babylon in 425 B.C.E. and the finishing of his book brings a period of history and our knowledge of what actually occurred in Judah to a close.

Nehemiah was a great supporter of Ezra; however, the story of Ezra's bringing of the Torah to Jerusalem differs drastically in the book attributed to him than the one recorded in the book of Ezra. The differences between these two versions exemplify a basic tension in Jewish life, and demonstrate the emergence of what I believe to be one of the core values of Jewish living embedded in our scriptures.

Ezra, or the book of Ezra, strongly supports the sacrificial system. In contrast, Nehemiah Chapter 8 affirms that the generation who built the Wall in Jerusalem under the leadership of Nehemiah, was governed by one desire, to explain the significance of the Torah. How were these two contrasting views reflected by their leadership styles?

Let's examine the texts in question.

The introductions to both chapters in Ezra and Nehemiah are similar. They both begin with the phrase,

> When the seventh month arrived, the children of Israel were in their cities and they all assembled in Jerusalem. (Ezra 3:1 and Nehemiah 7:73)

But from that point onward the text in Nehemiah reads differently.

Excerpts from Chapter 8:1-8 of Nehemiah:

> The entire people assembled as one man in the square before the Water Gate, and they asked Ezra the Scribe to bring the scroll of the Teaching of Moses with which the Lord had charged Israel. On the first day of the seventh

month, Ezra the priest brought the Teaching before the congregation, men and women and all who could listen with understanding. He read from it, facing the square before the Water Gate, from the first light until midday, to the men and the women and those who could understand; the ears of all the people were given to the scroll of Teaching.

Ezra the Scribe stood upon a wooden tower made for the purpose. He opened the scroll in the sight of all the people, for he was above all the people; as he opened it, all the people stood up. Ezra blessed the Lord, and all the people answered, Amen, Amen. With hands upraised. Then they bowed their heads and prostrated themselves before the Lord with their faces to the ground.

And the Levites explained the Teaching to the people, while the people stood in their places. They read from the scroll of the Teaching of God, translating it and giving the sense; so they understood the reading.

Nehemiah the Tirshatha, Ezra the priest and scribe and the Levites said to the people, "This day is holy to the Lord your God: you must not mourn nor weep" for all the people were weeping as they listened to the words of the Teaching. "Go, eat choice foods and drink sweet drinks and send portions to whoever has nothing prepared, for the day is holy to our Lord. Do not be sad, for your rejoicing is the source of your strength.

The book of Ezra records this public ceremony differently:

When the seventh month arrived-the entire people assembled as one man in Jerusalem. Then Joshua and his brothers built an altar of the God of Israel to offer burnt offerings upon it as it is written in the Teaching of Moses, the man of God. They set up the altar on its site because they were in fear of the peoples of the land, and they offered burnt offerings on it to the Lord, burnt offerings each morning and evening.

They celebrated the festival of Tabernacles as it is written, with its daily burnt offering in the proper quantities on each day as it is prescribed for it, followed by the regular burnt offering and the offerings for the new moons and for all the sacred fixed times of the Lord, and whatever freewill offerings were made to the Lord. From the first day of the seventh month, they began to make offerings to the Lord though the foundations of the Temple had not been laid. (Ezra 3:1-6)

Let's return to Nehemiah's version, and learn what occurred. Apparently a second assembly of all the people took place. It is recorded in Nehemiah 8:13-18.

> So the people went out and brought them, and made themselves booths on their roofs, in their courtyards, in the courtyards of the House of God, in the square of the Water Gate and in the square of the Ephraim Gate. The whole community that returned from the captivity made booths and dwelt in the booths-the Israelites had not done so from the days of Joshua son of Nun. And there was great rejoicing. He read from the scroll of the Teaching of God each day, from the first to the last day. They celebrated the festival seven days, and there was a solemn gathering on the eighth, as prescribed.

If we compare the two versions a number of discrepancies become apparent. Ezra is clearly concerned with sacrifice and Nehemiah doesn't even mention the altar.

The Nehemiah version understands the Levites to be teachers and interpreters of the law. Nehemiah emphasizes the learning of the Law of Moses rather than the observing the sacrifices which are mandated by the book of Leviticus.

The differences in the texts continue when they describe how the people observed the second day. Nehemiah indicates that the representatives of the people assembled, with the priests and Levites, around "Ezra the Scribe" to study the words of the Torah.

We read in Nehemiah:

> On the twenty-fourth day of this month the Israelites assembled, fasting in sackcloth, and with earth upon them. Those of the stock of Israel separated themselves from all foreigners and stood and confessed their sins and the iniquities of their fathers. Standing in their places, they read from the scroll of the Teaching of the Lord their God for one-fourth of the day. And for another fourth they confessed and prostrated themselves before the Lord their God.
>
> And on the platform of the Levites stood (a bunch of priests) and they cried in a loud voice, "Rise, Bless the lord your God who is from eternity to eternity: May your glorious name be blessed, exalted though is above every blessing and praise! (Nehemiah 9:1-5)

And then they recited Nehemiah's prayer which we also recite on the high holidays.

The differences in the two stories of Ezra bringing the Torah to Jerusalem raise an issue of serious importance. Nehemiah is supportive of Ezra's agenda but his text stresses that the study of the law and the presence of the Levites as the teachers of the law was the determining factor on that first Rosh Hashanah.

"Wow." Twenty –five hundred years ago, our people were concerned with what the message of the Law Giver or the message of the Torah should be. *Should it be a document which promoted a priesthood who offered sacrifices to God or should it be a document to be studied in order to assist a people to learn how they should conduct themselves in their daily lives?* It leaves us with a message and a basic question about the nature of leadership.

# ENDGAME

The Bible can be likened to an onion. It is composed of seemingly endless layers of wrappings with each layer holding a vital level of our story, a piece of wisdom. The more one peels away the layers, the more wisdom becomes apparent. The more layers, the more wisdom and depth.

The stories you have just read are part of series that I have been creating and field testing for several years. Each one is designed to bring to life less-known Biblical characters, to challenge us to consider the nature of their leadership, and reconsider our own styles of leadership in a volunteer organization. Each of us at times becomes a leader. How we lead in those situations influences how effective our organizations will be.

My own studies and my personal search for meaning have opened windows for me into ancient times and allowed the mythological personalities to be transformed into real people dealing with the personal and political issues of their times. In many ways we are alike. We, like them, are confronted with tasks and saddled with responsibilities. We, like them, are often placed in situations that demand leadership. Hopefully, the decisions we make will be good and effective even though we know these decisions are always open to criticism. Responding as wise leaders will enable us to continue to foster and encourage well run volunteer organizations in our communities. It is my hope that these examples will provide guidance when the need arises.

Rabbi Charles Simon
2015

FJMC and the Fischman family would also like to thank and acknowledge the following Regions, Clubs, and individuals for the support and love of our work.

## FJMC Builders

Beth Hillel Congregation B'nai Emunah Men's Club, Willmette, IL
Congregation Beth Israel Brotherhood, Worcester, MA
Congregation Beth Judea Men's Club, Long Grove, IL
The FJMC Florida Region
The FJMC Hudson Valley Region
The FJMC KIO Region
The FJMC Lake Ontario Region
The LDI Training Team 2012-14
The FJMC New England Region
The FJMC Seaboard Region
The FJMC Tri-State Region
The FJMC Western Region
Dr. Jerome & Estelle Agrest
Stephen Baum
Dr. Robert Braitman & Bonnie Gordon
Dr. Stephen H. Davidoff
Al & Helene Davis
Dr. Morris Diamont
Dr. Peter & Diane Gotlieb
Richard & Lillian Gray
Stan & Vanessa Greenspan
Peter Hodosh
Barbara Howarth
Allan & Helene Kahan
David Kaplan
Dr. Joel & Deborah Kurtz
Norm & Joan Kurtz
Arnold & Sharon Herman Miller
Donald & Regina Miller
Jeff & Elyse Schulman
Joel & Harriet Shrater
Charles Simon & Mary Katzin
Daniel & Sheila Stern
Warren & Adele Suffrin
Bob & Linda Watts
Eric & Fern Weis

## ABOUT THE AUTHOR

Rabbi Charles Simon is the Executive Director of the FJMC (Federation of Jewish Men's Clubs, Inc.) the male volunteer arm of Conservative/Masorti Judaism. He is the author of *Understanding Haftarot: An Everyperson's Guide* and the creator of The Unraveller an online weekly haftarah commentary. (Unraveller.org.). Perhaps more importantly for more than a decade he has demonstrated a commitment to build volunteer cultures, transforming synagogues into more inclusive venues, and studying how gender development and its relation to volunteerism.

## FJMC PUBLICATIONS & MATERIALS

FJMC publications are available through its website store at www.fjmc.org. Books marked with an asterisk * are available in electronic form (ex. – Kindle or Nook) through links on the FJMC site.

### Understanding The Haftarot: An Everyperson's Guide*
By Rabbi Charles Simon

"If the Haftarot are to reclaim their rightful place as a primary pedagogic tool for uncovering and imagining the Torah's deep truths for the modern synagogue attendee, then Rabbi Simon's exquisite, erudite and thorough introduction to the material offers an essential backdrop to each of us, clergy and layperson alike."

AARON ALEXANDER, DEAN ZIEGLER SCHOOL OF RABBINIC STUDIES AMERICAN JEWISH UNIVERSITY

### Understanding Ma'ariv: Book & Cd
Guide to leading and participating in the evening service. Includes full Hebrew text with musical notation side-by-side with English translation and transliteration.

### Understanding Havdalah: Book & Cd
Designed to teach anyone, even with minimal Hebraic skills, to chant Havdalah, the ceremony that separates Shabbat from the rest of the week. Includes full Hebrew text, translations and transliterations. Traditional music and the music of composer Debbie Friedman z'l.

## THE FJMC KERUV INITIATIVE SERIES

### Engaging The Non-Jewish Spouse: Strategies for Clergy and Lay Leadership
provides a step-by-step guide to inclusion taking into consideration the unique culture of each community. It suggests questions that should be discussed by a synagogue's leadership and serves as tool to further engage and guide a Board of Directors.

### Intermarriage: Concepts and Strategies for Families and Synagogue Leaders*
Does Keruv have an ideology and theology? And if so what is it? This is the most current thinking about intermarriage to date, an important read for family members and community leaders who wish to effectively work with intermarrieds or potential intermarrieds.

## HEARING MEN'S VOICES SERIES

### Jewish Men at the Crossroads*
This book addresses the many issues facing modern Jewish men, intermarriage, co-parenting, sexual dysfunction, retirement, and the evolving role of men.

### Hearing Men's Voices
Essays and programs designed to stimulate discussions and involvement in structured program activities directly related to issues confronting Jewish men. Books in the series are:

Work and Worth     Body and Spirit

Our Fathers/Ourselves     Listening to God's Voice

www.fjmc.org

# fjmc™

*Leadership - Innovation - Community*

The Federation of Jewish Men's Clubs' (FJMC) mission is to involve Jewish Men in Jewish Life by building and strengthening Men's Clubs in the Conservative/Masorti Movement. We accomplish this mission by:

> LEADERSHIP: mentoring leaders at the club, region and international level,
>
> INNOVATION: developing programming that better connects people of all ages to the Jewish community,
>
> COMMUNITY: forming meaningful long-lasting relationships based on camaraderie, common interests and core values.

The FJMC empowers its members, Jewish men and their families, to become more passionately engaged in Conservative/Masorti Jewish life. Its programmatic initiatives transform individuals and synagogues into more vibrant communities across the globe.

Website: www.fjmc.org
Facebook: FJMC_HQ
Twitter: @FJMC_HQ
LinkedIn: http://www.linkedin.com/company/fjmc

This book may not be reproduced, transmitted, or stored in whole or in part by any means, including graphic, electronic, or mechanical without the express written consent of the publisher except in the case of brief quotations embodied in critical articles and reviews.

Copyright © 2015 Federation of Jewish Men's Clubs, Inc.

ISBN
978-0-935665-09-3 – Paperback
978-0-935665-10-9 – E-book

Made in the USA
Lexington, KY
29 May 2015